[OFFICIAL COPY.]

AN EPITOME

OF THE

CHINO-JAPANESE WAR,
1894-95.

Compiled in the Intelligence Division of the War Office

BY

CAPTAIN N. W. H. DU BOULAY, R.A.

The Naval & Military Press Ltd

Reproduced by kind permission of the Central Library,
Royal Military Academy, Sandhurst

Published by
The Naval & Military Press Ltd
Unit 10, Ridgewood Industrial Park,
Uckfield, East Sussex,
TN22 5QE England
Tel: +44 (0) 1825 749494
Fax: +44 (0) 1825 765701
www.naval-military-press.com
www.military-genealogy.com

© The Naval & Military Press Ltd 2010

The Naval & Military Press ...

...offer specialist books for the serious student of conflict. The range of titles stocked covers the whole spectrum of military history with titles on uniforms, battles, official histories, specialist works containing Medal Rolls and Casualties Lists, and numismatic titles for medal collectors and researchers.

The innovative approach they have to military bookselling and their commitment to publishing have made them Britain's leading independent military bookseller.

In reprinting in facsimile from the original, any imperfections are inevitably reproduced and the quality may fall short of modern type and cartographic standards.

PREFACE.

In this short summary of the war between China and Japan political matters have been almost entirely omitted, and no reference has been made to the disturbances which arose in Korea during the course of the war. These disturbances no doubt caused anxiety to the Japanese commanders, but they did not materially affect the course of events.

The following authorities have been consulted:—

    Captain Cavendish's Reports.
    Captain Bower's Reports.
    Captain Du Boulay's Reports.
    Japanese Official Reports.
    " Problems of the Far East," by Hon. G. Curzon, M.P.
    " The China-Japan War," by Vladimir.
    " Revue Militaire de l'Etranger."

N. W. H. DU BOULAY, Capt., R.A.

9th July, 1896.

CONTENTS.

CHAPTER.	PAGE
I. Naval and military forces of China and Japan	7
II. Summary of events leading up to the war	17
III. Campaign in Korea and in southern Manchuria up to the commencement of December, 1894..	21
IV Port Arthur campaign	36
V. Events in Manchuria till the end of January, 1895	45
VI. Wei-hai-wei campaign	52
VII. Events in Manchuria from the commencement of February. Conclusion of the war	63
APPENDIX A. Strength and losses on both sides in the principal battles	73
,, B. Expenditure of ammunition by Japanese infantry in the principal battles	74
,, C. Expenditure of ammunition by the Japanese artillery in the principal battles	75
,, D. Movements of the head-quarters of the Japanese armies	76
,, E. Order of battle of the Japanese land forces	77

AN EPITOME

OF THE

CHINO-JAPANESE WAR,

1894-95.

CHAPTER I.

NAVAL AND MILITARY FORCES OF CHINA AND JAPAN.

THE Chinese navy [1] at the outbreak of the war was organized, as had been the case for many years, in four squadrons, namely, the Northern (Pei Yang), the Southern (Nan Yang), the Foochow, and the Canton squadron. Each squadron was under the control of a separate Provincial Governor, and there was no machinery for causing them to act together either as one fleet or in support of one another. The Northern or Pei Yang squadron was by far the most powerful of the four, and was the only one engaged in the war, though a few ships from other squadrons were added to it.

Chinese navy.

The ships of the Northern squadron were the following:—

    2nd Class battleships .. .. *Ting-yuen*
                                                  Chen-yuen

---

[1] "Problems of the Far East," pp. 358—360.

Armoured cruisers	*King-yuen*
	Lai-yuen
	Ping-yuen
3rd Class protected cruisers	*Chih-yuen*
	Ching-yuen
	Tsi-yuen
3rd Class unprotected cruisers	*Chao-yung*
	Yung-wei
Gunboats	Six built at Elswick, and known as the "Alphabetical gunboats."
Training ships	*Wei-yuen*
	Kang-chi
Torpedo boats	Thirteen (?)

And to these were added from other squadrons—

Despatch vessels	*Kuang-chia*
	Tsao-kiang
Transports	*Hai-ching*
	Tsche-hai
Torpedo gunboats	*Kuang-ping*
	Kuang-yi
Gunboat	*Mei-yuan*

In April, 1893, the complements of the ships of the Northern Squadron numbered 304 officers and 2,820 men. The younger officers were many of them well trained in their profession, and the men were generally well disciplined, but the senior officers—Captains, Commanders, and 1st Lieutenants—were, as a rule, very inefficient.

The two fortified harbours Port Arthur and Wei-hai-wei, with a first-rate dockyard at the former and workshops and stores at the latter, formed an excellent base for the Northern Squadron in carrying out its primary duty, namely, the defence of the approach to Peking.

Chinese army.

To describe the Chinese army before the war with anything approaching accuracy is impossible, since no reliable returns existed.

Each province of the Empire had a separate force at the disposal of its Governor, consisting of troops belonging to the four classes named below:— [1]

   a. Banner men.—These were the descendants of the army which conquered China and established the

---

[1] Japanese official reports.

Manchu dynasty 250 years ago. They included a certain proportion of Chinese who fought on the side of the conquerors, but were chiefly Manchus.

b. Green Standard troops.—These were a survival from the old Chinese army which was conquered by the Manchus.

c. Braves.—These were men voluntarily enlisted. They had their origin in Gordon's "ever victorious" army, and they superseded the Banner men and Green Standard troops for fighting purposes, these two classes having degenerated into inefficient local police.

d. Specially trained men of the Green Standard.— These were organised to supersede the Braves, since it was more economical to train men who were already receiving pay than to raise and pay others. At the beginning of the war, however, there were not very many of this class.

The Banner men (except those in Manchuria) and Green Standard troops were of no account for war. The other two classes were of equal, though small, value. They were armed with modern weapons, or at least had modern weapons in store, but had received very little training.

"Li-Hung-Chang's Army," which was composed of men of these two classes, was intended for coast defence round the Gulf of Pechihli. It had been well trained formerly, but had been deteriorating for many years, owing chiefly to Li-Hung-Chang's advancing age, which prevented him from taking the active interest in it which he had exhibited when it was first formed.

In his capacity as Viceroy of Chihli, Li-Hung-Chang also had at his disposal the rest of the provincial forces which were commanded by General Yeh. The troops at Peking, however, were not under his orders, but formed the Imperial Guard. About 13,000 of these (Banner men) formed the "Peking field force," originally organised after the 1860 war. They were armed with modern weapons, and passed as "foreign-drilled" troops on the strength of a course of instruction undergone by their predecessors at Tientsin from 1862 to 1865. [1]

---

[1] Captain Cavendish.

A scheme had been started in 1884 for training the troops in Manchuria as a defensive force. It was intended that in each of the three provinces 10,000 recruits should come up annually for a year's training, but at the time of the war with Japan this had only been carried out to a limited extent, though the few who had been trained were probably better troops than those in other parts of the Chinese Empire. [1]

No organized administrative services existed in the Chinese army, and during the war all arrangements for supply, and such medical services as were attempted, had to be improvised.

The following is a nominal distribution of the Chinese forces, though the actual numbers probably fell considerably below those given :—

		Banner men. (a)	Green Standard. (b)	Trained men. (c) and (d)	Total.
	Peking	125,160	10,000	28,270	163,430
	Coast defence, Chihli	1,070	8,090	28,150	37,310
	Rest of Chihli	17,040	16,280	10,560	43,880
	Total in Chihli	143,270	34,370	66,980	244,620
	Coast defence, Shantung	...	3,620	9,130	12,750
	Rest of Shantung	2,510	13,770	9,270	25,550
	Total in Shantung	2,510	17,390	18,400	38,300
Manchuria	Coast defence, Shingking	4,170	...	15,160	19,330
	Rest of Shingking	11,880	...	7,150	19,030
	Total in Shingking	16,050	...	22,310	38,360
	Total in Hei-lung-cheng (Tsitsihar)	8,080	...	8,040	16,120
	Total in Kirin	10,400	...	9,300	19,700
	Grand total in Chihli, Shantung, Manchuria.	180,310	51,760	125,030	357,100
	Total in rest of China	145,290	305,390	283,800	734,480
	Grand total for the Empire	325,600	357,150	408,830	1,091,580

[1] Japanese official reports.

The total of the trained men (*c* and *d*) in Chihli, Shantung and Manchuria included—
  92,390 Infantry.
  23,410 Cavalry.
  7,010 Artillery (field and garrison).
  1,090 Submarine miners.
  1,130 Boatmen, for work on canals and rivers.
The field artillery were armed with 7 cm. and 8 cm. Krupp field guns, but were very deficient in mobility and had hardly any training in gunnery.

The infantry were armed with rifles of various descriptions, both ancient and modern, Mausers, Remingtons, and Winchesters predominating. They had besides many native made rifles of 1-inch calibre, each carried and manipulated by two men.

There were no fixed terms of enlistment for the Chinese soldiers—

In China military rank is of no account, and the military profession is despised; it is not a matter for wonder therefore that the officers of the army were thoroughly inefficient, and spent their time in making schemes for their own pecuniary profit rather than in preparing themselves and their men for war.[1]

The Japanese navy was divided into three squadrons before the war, with head quarters respectively at the three naval ports—Yokosuka, Kure, Sasebo; but, unlike those of the Chinese navy, these three squadrons were under the control of the Central Government and were combined to form one fleet for the operations of the war.

Japanese navy

The following is a list of the Japanese ships at the beginning of the war:—

3rd Class battleship	*Fuso.*
1st Class cruisers, armoured	*Chiyoda.*
	Hiyei.
	Kongo.
	Riojo.
2nd Class protected cruisers	*Akitsushima.*
	Hashidate.
	Itsukushima.
	Matsushima.

---

[1] "Problems of the Far East," p. 353. Captain Cavendish.

2nd Class protected cruisers	*Naniwa.* *Takachiho.* *Yoshino.*
3rd Class cruisers	*Kaimon.* *Katsuragi.* *Musashi.* *Nishin.* *Takao.* *Tenriu.* *Tsukushi.* *Tsukuta.* *Yamato.* *Yayeyama* (despatch vessel).
Sloops	*Amagi.* *Seiki.*
Gunboats	*Akagi.* *Atago.* *Banjo.* *Chokai.* *Hosio.* *Iwaki.* *Maya.* *Oshima.*

As compared with the Chinese fleet, the Japanese ships had the advantage in speed and in their quickfiring armament; but none of them were equal in fighting power to the Chinese battleships *Ting-yuen* and *Chen-yuen*.

The Japanese had very good dockyards at Yokosuka, Kure, Sasebo,* and Nagasaki.

At the end of 1893 the *personnel* of the Japanese Navy was as follows :— [1]

---

[1] Japanese official reports.
* Near Nagasaki.

NAVAL AND MILITARY FORCES. 13

	Officers.	Warrant and Petty Officers.	Seamen	Cadets.	Civilians.	Total.
Serving afloat..	562	1,041	3,943	—	—	5,546
Serving ashore	593	914	4,181	175	1,013	6,876
Total serving	1,155	1,955	8,124	175	1,013	12,422
1st Reserve..	145	153	1,558	—	—	1,856
2nd Reserve	88	35	451	—	—	574
Grand total	1,388	2,143	10,133	175	1,013	14,852

As regards quality, it left little to be desired. It was well officered, well trained, and well disciplined, incontestably superior to that of the Chinese Navy.

The terms of enlistment were 4 years active service, 3 years in 1st Reserve, and 5 years in 2nd Reserve.

At the end of 1893 the strength of the Japanese Army was as follows:— (¹)

Japanese army.

	Generals and Field Officers.	Officers.	N.C.O.	Probationers and Cadets.	Soldiers.	Total.	Civilians.	Grand Total.
Peace establishment*	497	3,034	7,119	2,182	56,467	69,299	1,593	70,892
1st Reserve	127	460	3,870	—	87,795	92,252	—	92,252
2nd Reserve	56	294	1,756	—	103,914	106,020	—	106,020
Tondenhei†	9	82	291	—	3,671	4,053	51	4,104
Total	689	3,870	13,036	2,182	251,847	271,624	1,644	273,268

* The peace establishment and the 1st Reserve together constitute the 1st Line on a war footing.
† The military colonists of Yezo.

It was organized in six territorial Divisions, and one Imperial Guards Division. (²)

The territorial Divisions had each a peace strength of about 9,000 officers and men and a war strength of about 17,000.

The Guards Division had a peace strength of about

(¹) Japanese official reports.
(²) Captain Du Boulay.

8,000 and a war strength of about 13,000 officers and men.

Each Division was a complete unit in itself and comprised two infantry brigades, one artillery regiment,* one engineer battalion, one cavalry battalion, one train battalion, a medical corps, and an intendant, accountant, veterinary, and legal staff.

An infantry brigade had two regiments; and each regiment had three battalions† (except Guard regiments, which had only two).

The infantry were armed with the Murata rifle of 1889 pattern, a single loading breechloader of 8 mm. calibre. Each man carried 100 rounds of ammunition, and in reserve there were 30 rounds per rifle in the battalion transport and 50 in the divisional ammunition column. A new magazine rifle had been introduced, but was issued for service only to the Guard and 4th Divisions.

An artillery regiment had three "battalions" of two six-gun batteries each. Two battalions were field artillery, and the third mountain artillery. The guard artillery, however, had no mountain battalion.

The field gun was of compressed bronze with a breech action similar to Krupp's, calibre 2·95 inches; weight of projectile, 9 lbs. 5 ozs.; muzzle velocity, 1,417 f.s. 142 rounds a gun were carried with the batteries, and the same amount in the ammunition column.

The mountain gun was shorter than the field gun, but had the same calibre and fired the same projectile. The charge was smaller, and muzzle velocity 849 f.s. 144 rounds a gun were carried with the batteries, and the same amount with the ammunition column.

A cavalry battalion had two squadrons.‡

An engineer battalion had two field companies,§ and also formed bridging and telegraph sections, if required, on mobilization.

The train battalion furnished the *personnel*, ponies, &c., for all regimental and divisional transport.

The regimental transport consisted of pack ponies, each carrying about 250 lbs., and the usual subdivision into

---

* Corps artillery was specially formed during the war.
† A battalion at war strength has about 800 rifles.
‡ A squadron ,, ,, 100 sabres.
§ A field company ,, ,, 200 combatants.

light and heavy baggage was observed. The divisional transport, as normally organized, was also furnished by ponies, but this organization was modified, and during the war large use was made of hand-carts, each drawn by 3 coolies, and carrying from 300 to 400 lbs. Each division had three supply columns and five ammunition columns. Eight days' rations were carried in all.

The medical corps formed two bearer companies and six field hospitals.

The men of the 1st Reserve were utilized to augment units from peace to war strengths and to form depôts for each corps.

The men of the 2nd Reserves were mobilized territorially and formed additional units to be used for garrison work or on the lines of communications of an army in the field.

Besides the above, all men, medically fit, between the ages of 17 and 40 were liable to be called out on emergency to serve in the "National Army," which, however, had never been organized.

The terms of enlistment were 3 years with the colours, 4 years in the 1st Reserve, and 5 years in the 2nd Reserve.

The officers were carefully selected and thoroughly well trained, and the whole army was in an excellent state of discipline.

The Head-quarters of the Divisions were as follows:—

Guard Division	Tokio.
1st Division	Tokio.
2nd Division	Sendai.
3rd Division	Nagoya.
4th Division	Osaka.
5th Division	Hiroshima.
6th Division	Kumamoto.

The Japanese Headquarter Staff, which in peace time was located at Tokio, moved to Hiroshima at the beginning of the war, and thence directed operations. It included a Chief of the Staff for the army and one for the navy.*

---

* Admiral Kabayama.

working together directly under the Emperor, who was Commander-in-Chief of the land and sea forces. Subsequently, when it became necessary to move the Headquarter Staff to Port Arthur,* the office of Commander-in-Chief was delegated to Marshal Prince Komatsu, Chief of the Staff of the Army, and General Kawakami, formerly his assistant, became Chief of the Staff.

The conduct of the war by the Japanese was marked by a very complete decentralization. Commanders of armies or detached forces were given definite objectives (one at a time) by the Imperial Headquarter Staff, and were then allowed a free hand in carrying out their work —and the same system was followed within the armies and divisions.

Orders from Japan went by cable to Fusan and thence by telegraph to the 1st Army. For the 2nd Army, up till 30th December, orders were telegraphed to Ping Yang Inlet or Chemulpo, and thence taken by steamer to the Liaotung peninsula; but on the 30th December the telegraph line round the coast by Takushan and Pitzuwo to Chinchou was completed, so that from that time the 2nd Army was in direct telegraphic communication with Japan.

---

* See p. 70.

CHAPTER II.

SUMMARY OF EVENTS LEADING UP TO THE WAR. (¹)

UNTIL the summer of 1894 Korea had remained for hundreds of years unheeded and unknown by the Western world, except as an occasional source of differences between China and Japan.

Introductory.

The country had been for centuries closed against Europeans; and the failure of the French in 1866 and of the Americans in 1871 to exact reparation for the massacres of French and American subjects led the Koreans to think themselves invincible and to treat both Japanese and Chinese with contempt. But in 1875 this state of affairs was brought to an end. The Japanese in that year, in consequence of the murder of some Japanese sailors, made a naval demonstration against Korea, and obtained without fighting the signature of a Treaty opening the country to Japanese trade, and other foreign countries soon followed suit.

Opening of Korea to foreigners.

It is important to notice that in this, as in other instances, Japan dealt directly with Korea, ignoring the suzerainty claimed by China.

The opening of Korea led quickly to the establishment of large and flourishing Japanese settlements at Seoul, the capital, and at Chemulpo, Fusan, and Wonsan, and also to the formation of a party of progress amongst the Koreans. The leader of this party was Kim-Ok-Kiun, whilst the champion of the anti-foreign and anti-reform party was the Tai-Won-Kun, who had been appointed regent when the king was elected to the throne as a boy in 1864.

Results of the opening of Korea.

Two parties.

The Tai-Won-Kun had on his side the powerful Min faction, the followers of the queen, who occupied most of the high government positions, and he was no doubt also backed up by the Chinese Minister. Kim-Ok-Kiun on the other hand had the sympathies of the Japanese.

(¹) "The China-Japan War," by Vladimir.

(C.-J.W.) B

18　AN EPITOME OF THE CHINO-JAPANESE WAR.

Disturbances in 1882. In 1882 riots occurred at Sëoul, and the Japanese Minister had to fight his way to Chemulpo and escape to sea in a junk, whilst his Legation at Sëoul was burnt to the ground.

Chinese troops were on this occasion sent to Korea to put down the disturbances, and the Tai-Won-Kun was deported to China, where he remained for some years. The Japanese sent their Minister back to Sëoul with a military guard, and exacted reparation from Korea.

Disturbances in 1884. In December, 1884, another disturbance occurred, originated by Kim-Ok-Kiun, his plan being to assassinate the Min officials during a public dinner.

Prince Min-Yon-Ik was desperately wounded, and many of the other officials were killed during the night; and on the following day Kim-Ok-Kiun formed a new government and invited the Japanese to protect the king. The Min party however recovered from its first discomfiture, and obtaining the assistance of Chinese troops attacked the palace. During the fight that ensued the king fled, and the Japanese then retired to their Legation. Feeling was against them, and once more the Minister and his guard had to cut their way to Chemulpo, leaving their Legation in flames.

Tientsin Convention. The Japanese again exacted reparation from Korea; but on this occasion they had also to deal with China, since Chinese troops had been engaged against them. War between the two countries seemed imminent, but negotiations were opened which led to the signing of the Tientsin Convention* and the preservation of peace. By this convention it was agreed that both countries should withdraw their troops from Korea, and that if either country in the future found it necessary to send a force there again, the other country should receive notice of the intention to do so, and should be entitled to send a similar force.

Korea and her neighbours. This convention kept the peace in Korea for nine years, in spite of the conflicting interests of neighbouring Powers.

The Tonghaks. But in the spring of 1894 some disturbances arose in the southern provinces, which soon spread and increased to the proportions of a rebellion under the leadership of the Tonghaks, and ultimately led to the war between China and Japan.

---

* April 18th, 1885.

SUMMARY OF EVENTS LEADING UP TO THE WAR. 19

The Tonghak society was formed in 1859 by a man named Choi-chei-ou, who lived near Fusan. Its original object was the propagation of a new national religion, compounded from the doctrines and morals of Buddhism, Taoism, Confucianism, and Christianity; and its formation was therefore a movement against foreign teaching. Unfortunately the Korean Government could not discriminate between the Tonghaks and the Roman Catholics, and Choi-chei-ou was beheaded, in 1865, as a Roman Catholic. This of course exasperated the Tonghaks, and from that time the society became more political than religious, and added the overthrow of the Government to its other objects. It was not, however, strong enough by itself to attempt this at once, and had to wait till it could bring under its management the country people, who were generally in a state of chronic discontent and revolt against the existing maladministration.

In March, 1894, however, some local disturbances in the south gave the Tonghaks their opportunity, and they organised a widespread revolt. Part of the so-called Korean army was sent from Sëoul to suppress the rising, but though successful at first, the Government troops were decisively beaten on the 30th May, and forced to retire towards Sëoul. *Rebellion in spring of 1894.*

In this emergency the King of Korea applied to China for assistance, and Chinese troops were promptly sent to Asan, the first detachment leaving Wei-hai-wei on the 4th June and disembarking at Asan on the 8th, and others following a few days later. (¹) *Chinese assistance obtained.*

The Japanese Government had been informed of this despatch of troops in accordance with the terms of the Tientsin Convention, and determined to send a corresponding force. *Dispatch of Japanese troops.*

(²) On the 6th June, accordingly, orders were received by the general commanding the 5th Division at Hiroshima to prepare a brigade of all arms for service in Korea, and on the 9th June the first detachment of this brigade, consisting of an infantry battalion and some engineers, left Ujina, the port of embarkation, and sailed for Chemulpo. Having disembarked on the 12th June, the troops marched to Sëoul on the 13th, and relieved a party of

---

(¹) Captain Cavendish.
(²) Japanese official reports.

300 bluejackets who had escorted the Japanese minister, Otori, to the capital on the 10th.

The rest of the brigade followed at intervals, and by the end of June about 8,000 troops had landed at Chemulpo, most of them going on to Sëoul, and about 200 had landed at Fusan.

Major-General Oshima (commanding the 9th infantry brigade) was in command, and acted under instructions from Otori.

End of Tonghak rebellion. The Chinese troops in Korea at this time were all at Asan and numbered only 2,500; their arrival however had produced the desired effect upon the Tonghaks and had practically put an end to the rebellion.

Negotiations for withdrawal of Chinese and Japanese troops. Up to this point nothing had occurred to seriously endanger the preservation of peace between China and Japan. A simultaneous withdrawal of troops in accordance with the Tientsin Convention would have met the wishes of China; but the Japanese, who had important commercial interests involved, were unwilling to withdraw without some guarantee for the future peace, order, and good government of the country, and invited the Chinese to assist them in introducing certain reforms. The Chinese replied that measures of reform must be left to Korea herself, and refused to acknowledge the right of Japan to interfere.

The suzerainty of China over Korea was no doubt the point at issue; China refused to abandon it, and Japan considered that reforms in Korea were hopeless unless Chinese influence could be withdrawn.

Negotiations continued for some time, but it was evident that they were not likely to be successful, and both countries prepared to fight.

CHAPTER III.

CAMPAIGN IN KOREA, AND NAVAL BATTLE OF HAI-YANG-TAO (YALU).

AT the beginning of July, as stated above, the Japanese had a much stronger force of troops in Korea than the Chinese, and the latter therefore set to work during the progress of negotiations to redress the balance.

Chinese reinforcements during negotiations.

With this view 1,000 additional troops were sent to Asan; 3,500 crossed the Yalu and marched to Ping Yang; and 3,500 followed from Moukden. These northern troops were under the command of General Tso, the commandant of the Moukden province. (¹)

On the 20th July the Japanese minister addressed an ultimatum to the Korean Government insisting on the withdrawal of the Chinese troops. An unsatisfactory reply was received on the 22nd, and on the 23rd July the Japanese troops took possession of the royal palace, after a slight skirmish with the Korean guards.

Japanese ultimatum to Korea.

The first step taken by the Korean Government was to request the Japanese to drive the Chinese out of Korea; and, following upon this a mixed brigade under Oshima marched out of Sëoul on the 25th July to attack the Chinese at Asan, leaving a small force to guard the capital and to watch the road from Ping Yang.

Departure of Japanese troops from Sëoul for Asan.

(¹) Meanwhile, on the 22nd July, seeing that negotiations were practically at an end, the Chinese Government despatched reinforcements from Taku and Port Arthur to Korea by sea, escorted by men of war. 8,000 men were destined for Ping Yang, and 3,000 for Asan, the object of the Chinese Government being to strengthen the Asan garrison sufficiently to resist attack, and to collect a strong force at Ping Yang which should eventually drive the Japanese out of the country.

Further Chinese reinforcements.

The reinforcements for Ping Yang reached that place in safety on the 24th and 25th July, and about 1,800 men

---

(¹) Captain Cavendish.

22 AN EPITOME OF THE CHINO-JAPANESE WAR.

Naval action off Phungtao Island.

reached Asan on the 24th. But three Japanese cruisers—the *Yoshino*, *Naniwa*, and *Akitsushima*—had left Sasebo on the 23rd to intercept the Chinese reinforcements if possible, and these arrived in the neighbourhood of Asan early on the 25th.

The Chinese men-of-war, *Tsi-yuen* and *Kuang-yi*, which were acting as escort for the transports, steamed out of Asan Bay at daylight on the same day, in order to meet and escort the s.s. *Kowshing*, which was expected with the remaining 1,200 men; and, as they neared the island of Phungtao,* they came across the Japanese cruisers.

A short action ensued, but after keeping up the fight for about half-an-hour, the *Tsi-yuen* steamed off at full speed, followed somewhat cautiously by the *Yoshino*; and the *Kuang-yi* fled and was pursued by the *Naniwa*. The *Kuang-yi* ran ashore, was set on fire and abandoned, and the *Naniwa* then rejoined the *Akitsushima*.

Sinking of the s.s. Kowshing.

The Chinese despatch vessel *Tsao-kiang* and the s.s. *Kowshing* now appeared on the scene, and the *Akitsushima* at once gave chase to the former, and soon captured her. ([1])

The *Kowshing*,† in obedience to a signal from the *Naniwa*, stopped and anchored; and the captain of the *Naniwa* then sent a boat off with orders for the *Kowshing* to follow him. Captain Galworthy, the English captain of the *Kowshing*, agreed to do so under protest, but the Chinese officers on board his ship refused with threats to allow him. Finally at 1 p.m. the *Naniwa* opened fire, and about an hour later the *Kowshing* sank. In the confusion that arose on board the *Kowshing* when fire was opened, the Europeans jumped overboard, and the captain, first officer, a quartermaster, and Major von Hanneken,‡ who was a passenger, were eventually saved. Of the Chinese, over 1,000 lost their lives.

Battle of Sönghwan (Asan). ([2])

Whilst this encounter was taking place at sea, General Oshima's brigade was marching towards Asan. The

---

* Or Fontao.

† A steamer belonging to Messrs. Jardine, Matheson, and Co., and flying the English flag.

‡ A German military officer in the service of the Chinese Government.

([1]) "The China-Japan War," by Vladimir.

([2]) Japanese official reports.

CAMPAIGN IN KOREA AND IN SOUTHERN MANCHURIA. 23

Chinese under General Yeh* had moved forward from the place about 10 miles towards Sëoul, and had taken up a position on a ridge at Sönghwan; and the Japanese arrived in front of this position on the 28th, and prepared to attack it at daylight the following morning.

The attack was made in two columns, which moved off from their bivouac at midnight. The left or main column, consisting of about 2,000 infantry with 8 guns, was sent round the Chinese right flank, whilst the right column, 1,100 strong, made a demonstration against the Chinese front.

The Chinese made a short stand, but at 7 a.m. were in full retreat towards Asan. The Japanese however, who had few cavalry available, did not pursue w'· h any vigour, and when they reached Asan later in the d₹· the place was abandoned. The Chinese fled first of all to Kong-ju, and subsequently made their way by bye-roads, passing east of Sëoul to Ping Yang. The Japanese remained one day in Asan, and then returned to Sëoul, arriving there on the 5th August.

These two fights, one on land and one at sea, had taken place without any declaration of war, but on the 1st August war was declared by both countries. Declaration of war.

The Japanese now made preparations for driving the Chinese out of Korea, and on the 6th August the remainder of the 5th Division, under General Nodzu, landed at Fusan (except a small detachment which was taken round to Wonsan), and marched overland to Sëoul, arriving at the latter place towards the end of the month. Arrival in Korea of General Nodzu and rest of 5th Division. (¹)

General Nodzu himself reached Sëoul on the 19th August, and made his plans for a combined attack on Ping Yang, which was now held by the Chinese in force.

(¹) Ping Yang is a large walled town occupying a strong position on the right bank of the Tatung river, and was admirably situated as a place of concentration for the Chinese troops. These now consisted of 3,500 men under General Tso from the Moukden province, 1,500 under Fengshenga from Moukden, 6,000 under General Wei from Chihli, 2,000 under Ma-yü-kun from Port Arthur, Ping Yang.

---

* Commanding troops of Chihli province. He had with him also General Nieh-ssŭ-chêng, commanding troops in North Chihli.
(¹) Japanese official reports.

and 1,000 under General Yeh from Asan,* making a total of 14,000. General Yeh was in chief command.

The place had been strengthened with earthworks, and a bridge of boats had been constructed across the river, protected by several strong works on the left bank.

Skirmish at Chunghua.(¹) On the 13th August a force of 1,500 Chinese surrounded and cut up a small Japanese reconnoitring party at Chunghua, and then advanced southwards as far as Hwang-ju.

Disposition of Japanese troops. (¹) After his return from Asan, General Oshima had moved north with most of his brigade† to Phyong-san, detaching three companies to Sak-riöng.

The Sak-riöng detachment was increased in the middle of August by the arrival of a battalion, a battery, and a troop of cavalry which had landed at Wonsan, and it was eventually put under the command of General Tachimi. The rest of the 5th Division was in and near Séoul under the immediate command of General Nodzu; and in addition to his own Division he had at his disposal a detachment of the 3rd Division, consisting of 3 battalions, 2 mountain batteries, 1 troop of cavalry, and 1 company of engineers, under General Sato, which landed at Wonsan on the 26th and 27th August, just in time to take part in the operations.

General Nodzu's plan of attack. (¹) General Nodzu's first plan was to send Oshima against Ping Yang by the main road, whilst all the other columns, including Sato's troops at Wonsan, should move round the Chinese left and attack from the north-east and north. But this plan was afterwards changed, and the main column, under Nodzu himself, was taken across the Tatung river near Hwang-ju, to attack from the west.

It was arranged that the combined attack should be made from all sides on the 15th September, and it was left to the several commanders to bring their detachments within striking distance by that day.

Intercommunication between Oshima's brigade and the columns on his right was almost impossible, owing to the hilly nature of the intervening country and the absence of roads, and until the afternoon of the 14th September General Nodzu was ignorant of the whereabouts of the Sak-riöng and Wonsan detachments.

---

* General Nieh had returned to Tientsin for reinforcements.
† 9th.
(¹) Japanese official reports.

On the 14th September, as there had been some delay in crossing the Tatung, and the greater part of the main column was therefore a day behind time, General Nodzu sent orders to Oshima to engage the enemy's attention on the 15th, but to postpone the real attack till the following day. General Oshima, in acknowledging the receipt of the order, pointed out that in all probability the Wonsan and Sak-riöng detachments would attack on the 15th as previously arranged, and that if this were the case he would feel bound to give them all the assistance he could, especially as the main column would be unable to co-operate.

General Nodzu's orders on 14th September.

(¹) On the 15th September General Oshima opened fire with his guns at daylight, and sent his infantry forward against the Chinese works on the left bank of the river. One work was carried at once, but the others proved too formidable, and the want of intercommunication between the columns then made itself felt.

Battle of Ping Yang.

Sato* and Tachimi, who had arrived within striking distance of Ping Yang to the north, hearing the firing, and having received no order to postpone the attack, at once sent their men forward to engage the enemy, who was occupying a line of works north of the town; and Oshima in his turn, hearing the firing to the north, concluded that the two northern detachments were attacking, and felt it his duty to push his own attack with the utmost vigour. The result was that he lost heavily, and had to retire to his former positions in the afternoon.

The northern detachments carried the works in front of the town, but then found themselves face to face with the walls of Ping Yang itself, which offered an apparently insurmountable obstacle to further progress.

The troops were therefore withdrawn to a safe distance to await a more favourable opportunity.

Of the main column only the advanced guard had arrived on the scene, and it was unable to effect anything of importance against the Chinese fortifications. It had succeeded, however, in heading off and annihilating two bodies of Chinese cavalry which tried to escape to the westward.

---

* Sato had attacked and occupied Shu-nan on 13th September.

(¹) Japanese official reports.

The prospects of the Japanese, therefore, in the early part of the afternoon were by no means promising; but at 4 p.m. the Chinese displayed white flags on the walls at the northern end of the town and offered to surrender.

In the negotiations, such as they were, which followed, the Chinese obtained a postponement of the actual surrender till the following morning, and then utilized the darkness of night to escape *en masse* to the north, between the Wonsan detachment and the main column.

The Japanese entered the abandoned town on the 16th September, sending a small force in pursuit of the Chinese as far as the Chongchon river.

Their losses on the 15th were 189 killed and 516 wounded, of whom 130 killed and 290 wounded belonged to Oshima's brigade.

The Chinese killed numbered about 2,000. General Wei, with part of his force, had anticipated the advance of the Japanese and retired towards the Yalu before the attack, and for this conduct he was subsequently beheaded.

General Tso is said to have fought most bravely, and died fighting.

General Ma-yŭ-kun, with the Port Arthur contingent, opposed General Oshima's brigade.

Arrival of General Katsura and rest of 3rd Division in Korea; and formation of 1st Army. Meanwhile, on the 12th September, the Japanese forces in Korea were increased by the arrival at Chemulpo of the remainder of the 3rd Division under General Katsura, and the two divisions, 3rd and 5th, henceforth formed the 1st Army, under the command of Marshal Yamagata.

Naval operations subsequent to 25th July. Two days after the battle of Ping Yang, that is on the 17th September, the naval battle of Hai-yang-tao, frequently called the battle of the Yalu, was fought; and the movements of the two fleets subsequent to the action of the 25th July will now be described.

For some time nothing remarkable was done on either side. The Chinese fleet remained inactive at Wei-hai-wei, probably because it was not yet ready to fight, and the Japanese fleet which had to cover the movements of the transports found its task a simple one.

On 10th August 19 Japanese ships appeared off Wei-hai-wei, exchanged a few shots with the forts at long range, and then disappeared again.

On 17th August the Chinese fleet steamed round from Wei-hai-wei to Taku for stores, returning again on the

19th, but otherwise the ships only left the harbour for short cruises.

On the 12th September, however, in obedience to orders from Tientsin, Admiral Ting took his fleet to Port Arthur to make arrangements for convoying troops from Talienwan to Takushan. His intention was to seek out and fight the Japanese fleet so as to leave the route clear for the transports, and accordingly, on the receipt of a telegram on the 13th informing him that two Japanese cruisers had appeared off Wei-hai-wei, he at once put to sea and steamed across to the Shantung promontory, sending two cruisers to scout to the south. Nothing however was seen of the Japanese fleet, and the Chinese ships returned to Wei-hai-wei o.. the 14th for news, and proceeded to Talienwan at 11 p.m. the same day.

On arrival at Talienwan before noon on the 15th September they found that five transports had come in shortly before with troops on board from Taku.

News was received during the day of the Japanese victory at Ping Yang, and additional soldiers* were therefore hurriedly put on board the transport ready to start at 2 a.m. the next morning.

The fleet left at 1 a.m. on the 16th and shaping a course eastward of the direct line, reached Tatungkan 2 p.m., about the same time as the transports, which had started later but had gone direct to their destination.

Two gunboats and two torpedo boats were sent into the river to assist in the disembarkation; and the troops were all landed during the afternoon.

The Japanese fleet, under Vice-Admiral Ito, after making the reconnaissance at Wei-hai-wei on the 10th August, returned to the neighbourhood of Korea to cover the operation of transporting the main parts of the 3rd Division from Japan to Chemulpo. This was completed, as already stated, on the 12th September, and on the 14th the fleet moved northwards to the Tatung river (Ping Yang inlet), leaving six ships to guard the transports at Chemulpo.

Three gunboats and some torpedo boats were sent up the Tatung to assist the army, and on the 16th September

---

* About 2,500 came from Taku, and about 1,500 embarked at Talienwan (?).

the rest of the fleet put to sea to try and intercept the Chinese transports, which it was known were taking reinforcements to the Yalu.*

Naval battle of Hai-Yang-tao (Yalu).

At daylight on the 17th September the fleet reached Hai-yang-tao Island, and steaming thence in a north-easterly direction, discovered the Chinese fleet at 11.30 a.m., and forming single line ahead, advanced to the attack.

The Chinese ships were at anchor, ten in deep water, two just outside the mouth of the river, and two gunboats and two torpedo boats in the river itself; but as soon as the smoke of the Japanese fleet was observed to the south-west, Admiral Ting made the signal to weigh, and ordered the gunboats in the river to rejoin the fleet. The ships then formed somewhat irregularly in line abreast, with the two battleships in the centre, and gradually wheeled to starboard, so that their line should be parallel with that of the Japanese ships, which were advancing diagonally across the front of the Chinese and making for their right flank. Fire was opened from the 30·5-cm. guns of the *Ting-yuen* at a range of 6,000 yards, but the Japanese did not reply till the range was reduced to 3,000 yards.

The Japanese fleet was organized in two squadrons. The flying squadron consisting of 4 cruisers, and the main squadron consisting of the rest of the fleet, namely, 6 ships, one gunboat and one armed transport. The flying squadron led the line, and, as the two squadrons successively passed the Chinese right, they succeded in sinking the *Chao-yung* and in setting fire to the *Yung-wei*, which was taken out of the action and eventually beached.

The Japanese ship *Hiyei*, which could not keep up with the main squadron, had to break through the Chinese line, and suffered considerably. She was, however, supported by the gun vessel *Akagi*, until the flying squadron came to their assistance, and they were both able to withdraw out of range.

Whilst the Japanese squadrons were still engaged on the Chinese right, two ships on the left, the *Kuang-chia* and *Tsi-yuen*, took the opportunity of escaping altogether; and two others, the *King-yuen* and *Chih-yuen*, which had advanced by themselves in front of the general Chinese line, were shortly afterwards sunk by the fire of

---

* The whereabouts of the Chinese fleet was not definitely known. (Japanese official report.)

the main Japanese squadron. The ten Chinese ships which began the fight were now therefore reduced to four, namely, the *Ting-yuen* and *Chen-yuen* battleships, and the *Lai-yuen* and *Ching-yuen* cruisers; and the ships at the mouth of the river had failed to join the rest of the fleet. The twelve Japanese ships had likewise been reduced to ten by the withdrawal of the *Akagi* and the *Hiyei*; and the armed transport *Saikio Maru* had also steamed away, leaving nine ships to the Chinese four.

The *Saikio Maru* had been directed to keep out of danger as much as possible, but seeing the *Yung-wei* trying to escape, she had gone off in pursuit; she was then herself attacked by the Chinese inshore squadron, but escaped any serious injury, and proceeded in safety to the Ping Yang inlet.

The two fleets, thus reduced in numbers, continued the fight, which was now at its hottest; and after a time the *Ching-yuen* and *Lai-yuen* both caught fire and steamed away westwards, pursued by the Japanese flying squadron. This left the main squadron engaged with the two Chinese battleships, but though the fighting was continued till dusk, no decisive result was obtained.

Just before dark the flying squadron was recalled, and the Japanese fleet drew off from the Chinese ships in order to avoid any danger from the Chinese torpedo boats in the darkness.

The two Chinese battleships followed the Japanese for a short time, and then steered for Port Arthur, and the Japanese then steered a parallel course, intending to continue the fight the next morning. But at daylight the Chinese ships were nowhere to be seen, and the Japanese fleet returned to the Ping Yang inlet, arriving early on the 19th September.

The Chinese, in addition to 700 killed and 200 or 300 wounded, had lost five ships, the *Yung-wei*, *Chao-yung*, *King-yuen*, *Chih-yuen*, and *Kuang-chia*; the last named, after escaping from the fight, ran ashore near Talienwan, and became a total wreck; and the *Ting-yuen*, *Chen-yuen*, *Lai-yuen*, *Ching-yuen*, *Ping-yuen*, and *Tsi-yuen* all required considerable repairs, which were taken in hand at Port Arthur.

The Japanese had 80 killed and 162 wounded, of whom 51 killed and 41 wounded belonged to the flagship *Matsu-*

shima. They lost no ships, but the *Matsushima, Hiyei,* and *Akagi* had to return to Japan for repairs.

This battle practically gave the Japanese command of the sea, for even after the Chinese ships had been repaired, they did not venture out of harbour again. At the same time the Japanese continued to act with great caution, for the Chinese battleships had shown their superior fighting power, and the general condition of the Chinese fleet could not be accurately known.

Concentration of Chinese army at the Yalu.

The Chinese after their defeat at Ping Yang retreated to the Yalu.* (¹) General Sung, the commandant of Port Arthur, had already taken up a position on the right bank near Chiuliencheng with a force of about 11,000 men;† and the army now united under his command numbered about 20,000. There was also a force of 4,500 under I-ko-teng-a (of Tsitsihar), 10 miles higher up the river.

Battle of Hushan and passage of the Yalu by the Japanese.

The main part of the Japanese 1st Army remained echeloned between Ping Yang and the Chongchon river till the 5th October, during which time supplies from Japan were landed at the Ping Yang inlet, which became the principal base, and were forwarded along the road to the north.

The advanced guard‡ under General Tachimi pushed forward from the Chongchon river on the 6th October and arrived at Wiju, on the left bank of the Yalu opposite Chiuliencheng, on the 10th; the main body (¹) followed from the Chongchon on the 15th October and reached Wiju on the 23rd, the line of communications from Ping Yang to the Chongchon being guarded by a mixed brigade under General Oshima.§

---

* 5,000 under Machin-sü, who took Wei's place.
2,000 under Nieh-kuei-lin, who succeeded Tso.
1,000 under Fengshenga.
1,000 under Ma-yü-kun.

Total 9,000 approximately.

† Partly collected from Mukden province, Yingtzu, &c., and partly sent by sea from Port Arthur, Talienwan, and Taku, under Nieh-ssŭ-chêng.

‡ The China-Japan War—Vladimir.

§ Commanding 6th brigade, not the Oshima who fought at Sönghwan and Ping Yang.

(¹) Japanese official reports.

Just above Chiulienchèng a tributary stream, the Ai-ho, joins the Yalu from the north, and in the angle formed by the two rivers stands a prominent hill called Hushan.

The Chinese held this hill as an advanced position in front of their left flank, their main position extending along the right bank of the Yalu from Chiulienchêng to Antung. In front of this main position the river was broad and deep, and the country on the opposite bank was flat and open, and Marshal Yamagata, realising the difficulty of making a direct attack, determined to capture Hushan first, and then fording the tributary stream to turn the Chinese left. The attack was arranged to take place at daylight on the 25th October.

The chief difficulty which presented itself was the crossing the main stream of the Yalu, which at that time of year was 11 feet deep, and a little more than 200 yards wide. On the one hand, the bridge had to be constructed by night, on account of the presence of the Chinese, and on the other, the pontoon equipment with the army was insufficient, and the water was so bitterly cold that the men, who had to stand in it, could only work in very short reliefs.

However, the difficulties were successfully overcome, and the Chinese found themselves unexpectedly attacked at Hushan in the early morning of the 25th October, and abandoned their position at 8 a.m. The defenders of the main position then seemed to wake up, and two separate forces advanced to recapture Hushan, one marching from Chiuliencheng and the other crossing the tributary stream higher up and moving towards Hushan from the north.

The Japanese advanced troops were in some difficulty for a time, but reinforcements were brought across the bridge as quickly as possible, and by 10.30 a.m. the Chinese were completely defeated and driven back across the Ai-ho, followed by the Japanese, who bivouacked for the night on its right bank above Chiuliencheng.

A detachment of the Japanese army under Colonel Sato had been ordered to cross the Yalu nine miles above Wiju on the 24th, and to move down the right bank on the 25th so as to assist the rest of the army. This detachment met with hardly any opposition from the troops under I-ko-teng-a, but it was too late to take any part in the main battle.

On the following morning, 26th October, the Japanese

entered Chiuliencheng and Antung, which had been evacuated by the Chinese during the night.

The Japanese losses were 34 killed and 111 wounded, and about 500 Chinese dead were counted, though probably many more were carried down the river.

Part of the Chinese army retreated to the north-east, part to Fenghuangcheng, and the rest to Hsiu-yen and beyond.

Movements of Japanese after the passage of the Yalu.

(¹) The 1st Japanese Army had now completed its allotted task of driving the Chinese out of Korea, and before undertaking any further advance of importance it had to await the result of the operations of the 2nd Army, which landed in the Liao-tung peninsula on the 24th October to attack Port Arthur. But in the meantime columns were sent forward along the several roads towards Mukden, Haicheng, and Port Arthur, to reconnoitre and prepare for a future advance, and this led to a number of small encounters with the Chinese.

Occupation of Fenghuangchêng.

(¹) On 29th October the 10th brigade, under General Tachimi, entered Fenghuangchêng without fighting, the Chinese having retired partly to the Motienling pass, and partly to Hsi-muchêng.

Occupation of Takushan and Hsiu-yen.

(¹) On the 30th October two columns from the 3rd Division left Antung by different roads for Takushan, which they reached on the 7th November without meeting any resistance, and the combined force marched on, a few days later, towards Hsin-yen, whilst a battalion of the 13th Brigade approached by the direct road from Fenghuangchêng. The Takushan column had two slight skirmishes on the 16th and 17th November, and both columns entered Hsiu-yen on the 19th, the Chinese, who numbered about 3,000, retreating towards Hsi-muchêng when they found themselves threatened from the two sides.

The object of this advance was to clear the Chinese troops away from the neighbourhood of Takushan, which was intended to become an auxiliary base for the future advance to Haicheng; but as there was found to be considerable difficulty in immediately supplying a large force at Hsiu-yen, the troops were all withdrawn on the 23rd November except one battalion.

(¹) Japanese official reports.

The battalion of the 10th brigade returned to Fenghuangchêng, and the remainder to Takushan.

Kwimpo, near the mouth of the Yalu, was also used as an auxiliary base as soon as the Japanese had crossed that river.

But the Ping Yang inlet still remained the principal base for the 1st Army, and when the winter set in, in the middle of December, Kwimpo and Takushan were closed by ice,* and all stores had to be forwarded over land from the inlet.

General Tachimi meanwhile had been engaged in several small fights beyond Fenghuangchêng. Skirmishes north and north-east of Fenghuangchêng.

On the 13th November a battalion of his brigade, reconnoitring along the main road to Liaoyang and Mukden, reached the neighbourhood of the Motienling pass and had a slight skirmish, which showed that the pass was strongly held by the Chinese. Other Chinese troops were also reported to be advancing from the north-east and east, and the battalion therefore retired to Tsao-ho-kou, where it was reinforced by another battalion, a squadron of cavalry, and a battery, under Colonel Tomioka.

Skirmishes also took place between reconnoitring parties from both sides in the country between Tsaimasui, Ai-yang-ping-men, and Fenghuangchêng on the 13th, 17th, and 19th November, and a Japanese patrol was attacked at Kuan-tien by a Chinese force from Ai-yang-ping-men on the 21st November.

As these encounters showed that the Chinese were in considerable force in that direction, General Nodzu made arrangements to clear them out by a combined movement on Tsaimasui.

Two battalions and one battery under Colonel Nishijima were to advance from Chiulienchêng, and after dispersing the enemy at Kuan-tien, thence continue their march to Tsaimasui; one infantry regiment, one squadron, and one battery, under Colonel Tomoyasu, were to advance by the direct road from Fenghuangchêng; and the greater part of Colonel Tomioka's force was to advance from Tsao-ho-kou.

The Chinese, however, were at the same time planning

---

* Kwimpo was again full of ice on 7th March, and Takushan a few days after.

a combined attack from Tsaimasui and Motienling on the Japanese force at Tsao-ho-kou; and as this attack was made on the 25th November, Colonel Tomioka was prevented from taking the part assigned to him in the Japanese plan of operations, and had to content himself with repulsing the forces which attacked him. The other two Japanese columns reached Tsaimasui with little opposition, and finding that the Chinese had collected, 30 miles north-east of Tsao-ho-kou, continued their march in that direction, and inflicted a severe defeat upon them on the 30th November.

After this the Japanese troops were withdrawn to the neighbourhood of Fenghuangchêng.

Distribution of Japanese troops at the beginning of December.

The Japanese in Manchuria were now distributed as follows:—(¹)

Headquarters of 1st Army,
Headquarters of 3rd Division,
    Part of 5th brigade,
    6th brigade,
} at Antung.

Remainder of 5th brigade at Takushan, with 1 battalion at Hsiu-yen.

Headquarters of 5th Division,
9th brigade,
} at Chiulienchêng.

10th brigade at Fenghuangchêng.

Summary of Chinese movements.

The movement of the Chinese after their defeat on the Yalu are somewhat difficult to trace, but were approximately as follows:—(²)

General I-ko-teng-a with 4,000 men, who had opposed Colonel Sato's crossing, retired in a north-easterly direction.

General Sung with 5,000 men and Ma-chin-hsü with 5,000 retired to Fenghuangchêng.

General Feng-sheng-a, and General Nieh-kuei-lin (who succeeded General Tso), retired to Hsiu-yen and the passes west of it, with 3,000 men.

The rest of the army probably dispersed.

When the Japanese advanced to Fenghuangchêng, General Sung retired to the Motienling pass, and General Machin-sü to Hsi-muchêng; and when Hsiu-yen was

---

(¹) Japanese official reports.
(²) Captain Cavendish, and Japanese official reports.

captured, Generals Feng and Nieh-kuei-lin fell back on Hsi-muchêng and joined General Machin-sü there.

On the 9th November General Sung, with Ma-yü-kun as chief of his staff, left his troops at Motienling under Nieh-ssŭ-chêng, and picking up 2,000 Honan* men at Haicheng, went southwards by Kai-ping to attack the Japanese 2nd Army, which was reported to be marching on Port Arthur.†

General I-ko-teng-a on retiring towards Kirin took command of a fresh force of 10,000 men, and returned again to the front, and it was the advanced guard of his troops which was engaged with Tachimi in the country north and north-east of Fenghuangchêng.

The forces opposing the Japanese in Manchuria at the beginning of December were therefore— _{Disposition of Chinese forces at the beginning of December.}

10,000 under I-ko-teng-a to the north and north-east of Fenghuangchêng.

5,000 under Nieh-ssŭ-chêng at Motienling.

7,000 under Feng-sheng-a, Nieh-kuei-lin, and Machin-sü at Hsi-muchêng.

It may be mentioned that General Yeh, who had been honoured for his "masterly retreat" from Asan, was now on his way to Peking to appear before the Board of Punishment. He had been denounced by General Sung for misconduct at Ping Yang and the Yalu, and the real truth about Asan had also reached the ears of the authorities at Peking. He was finally sentenced to death, but not till 1896.

---

* 2,400 were sent to Haicheng from Yingtzu on 26th October.

† Sung's movement appears to have been unknown to the Japanese 1st Army. No co-operation of the two armies seems to have been intended before January, 1895. See p. 49.

CHAPTER IV.

PORT ARTHUR CAMPAIGN. ([1])

Formation of 2nd Army.

THE naval battle of Hai-yang-tao gave the Japanese the command of the sea, at any rate for a time, and they determined to follow up their victory by the attack and capture of Port Arthur with its dockyard, which would deal another blow at Chinese naval power, and would provide a convenient base for future operations against Peking.

For this purpose the 2nd Army* was organised under Marshal Oyama, consisting of the 1st Division, commanded by General Yamaji, a mixed brigade of the 6th Division, commanded by General Hasegawa, and a siege train. Hasegawa's brigade left Japan between the 26th and 28th September, and landed at Chemulpo as a temporary support for the 1st Army. The headquarters of the 2nd Army and 1st Division having embarked at Ujina in 33 ships on the 16th October and following days, sailed to the Ping Yang inlet, and there remained till the 23rd October.

* Approximate strength of 2nd Army:—

	Officers and men.	Coolies, and Soldiers employed as coolies.	Total.
1st Division	15,000	4,750	19,750
Hasegawa's brigade†	7,560	1,000	8,560
Line of communications troops	2,000	7,000	9,000
Siege train ‡	1,000	—	1,000
Staff	160	150	310
TOTAL	25,720	12,900	38,620

† 12th Infantry brigade with two mountain batteries, one squadron, one company engineers, &c., attached.
‡ Six companies, specially formed from the coast artillery. For armament, see p. 77.

([1]) Japanese official reports, and Captain Du Boulay.

The Ping Yang inlet was being used at this time as the headquarters of the Japanese fleet. Admiral Ito had contented himself with keeping a watch on the movements of the Chinese ships, reconnoitring the coasts of Shingking and Liaotung for a landing place, and escorting transports from Japan to Korea. For all these purposes individual ships were used, the main part of the fleet remaining concentrated in the Ping Yang inlet. *[Movements of the fleets.]*

The Chinese fleet had returned to Port Arthur for repairs after the battle of Hai-yang-tao, and about the 20th October six ships put to sea and went over to Wei-hai-wei, but there was apparently no intention of again trying conclusions with the Japanese.

There was very little fear, therefore, of interference by the Chinese with the movements of the Japanese transports, and on the 23rd October, in the evening, the first convoy of 16 ships steamed across from Ping Yang Inlet to a point on the Chinese coast at the mouth of the Hua-yüan river.* *[Disembarkation of 1st Division.]*

They were accompanied by 9 or 10 Japanese men-of-war as escort, whilst the rest of the fleet proceeded to the Elliot Islands and kept a look-out for the Chinese ships.

The disembarkation was commenced at daylight on the 24th October, and the other transports arrived next morning. As the ships were unloaded they went back to Chemulpo in order to bring over General Hasegawa's brigade.

The landing place was not a good one, as the ships had to lie off about $3\frac{1}{2}$ miles from the shore, and the mud was uncovered at low tide for a distance of 3 miles, but it was the best place that could be found on that part of the coast.

The disembarkation was not interrupted by the Chinese, and a small advance guard was sent forward on the 25th October toward Pitzuwo, followed by the rest of the 1st Division on the 1st November.

A glance at the map will show that the natural place for the Chinese to make a stand for the defence of Port Arthur was near Chinchou,† where a narrow isthmus separates Talienwan Bay from Society Bay. A position on this isthmus could not be easily turned, because on the one side Society Bay is very shallow, and on the other *[Chinese defensive arrangements.]*

---

* Long. 122° 41' E; Lat. 39° 31½' N.
† Or Kin-chow.

Talienwan Bay was defended by 6 forts armed with modern Krupp and Creuzot guns.

The garrison of Chinchou and the Talienwan forts was about 6,500 men at the beginning of the war; 1,500 of these had left for Takushan on the 15th September,* but on the other hand the garrisons of Kaiping and Fuchou, numbering about 1,000, had been moved southwards to take their place, and at the time of the Japanese attack the defenders numbered about 6,000.

The original garrison of Port Arthur was 7,750 men. 2,000, however, had left for Ping Yang under command of General Ma-yü-kun, about the 23rd July,† and the number was thus reduced to 5,750, commanded by no less than 7 generals of equal rank;‡ but reinforcements arrived by sea on the 3rd and 6th November, bringing the strength of the garrison up to 10,800 men; and, before the Japanese attacked, General Chieng had been given the chief command. (¹)

Chinchou itself was held by the Chinese. It is a large walled town, but is commanded by hills within easy artillery range to the north and north-east, and the Chinese would have done better either to have fallen back about two miles to the narrowest part of the isthmus, or to have gone forward and held some of the numerous defensive positions commanding the road from Pitzŭwo.

Movements of Chinese fleet after disembarkation of 2nd Army.

The Chinese fleet took no part in the defence of either Talienwan or Port Arthur. It arrived at the latter place from Wei-hai-wei at the beginning of November, but in obedience to orders from Tientsin returned again on the 7th. On the 9th November it went to Taku for stores, and once more returned to Wei-hai-wei on the 12th. The Japanese fleet made no attempt to intercept either the Chinese men-of-war or the Chinese transports, but remained quietly amongst the Elliot Islands, allowing them to come and go as they liked, provided they did not interfere with the Japanese transports.

Capture of Chinchou.

By the evening of the 5th November the Japanese troops were within a few miles of Chinchou. The greater part

---

* See footnote p. 27.
† See p. 19.
‡ General Sung, the Commandant, had left for the Yalu.
(¹) Captain Cavendish.

of the Division had moved across country from the Pitzŭwo road to Suanshilipu, on the main road from Fuchou to Chinchou; but one regiment of infantry, one mountain battery, and one squadron of cavalry were left on the Pitzŭwo road fronting two small works which were held by the Chinese.

On 6th November these two works were carried at daybreak without trouble, and the column pushed on to take part in the attack on Chinchou, which was to be made simultaneously by both roads.

The attack began by an advance of the Japanese infantry along the Fuchou road against a position held by the Chinese some 2,500 yards in front of the town. The Chinese at once retired, and the position was occupied by the Japanese artillery, which opened fire at 9 a.m. against the town itself, the mountain battery on the Pitzŭwo road co-operating at a closer range.

The 2nd infantry regiment* meantime advanced over the hills on the right of the artillery, and at 10 a.m. were approaching the north wall of Chinchou, whilst the 3rd regiment, keeping still further westward, advanced between Chinchou and the sea.

The Chinese at once began to stream away to the south, and at 11.15 a.m. the 2nd regiment entered the town by the north gate, which was blown in with gunpowder, whilst the rest of the Japanese army pursued the retreating Chinese.

On the following day, the 7th November, all the Talienwan forts fell into the hands of the Japanese without a shot being fired, the defenders escaping towards Port Arthur, and the Japanese fleet which approached the bay in the early morning to co-operate in the attack found the forts already occupied by the army and the Japanese flag flying over them. {Occupation of Talienwan.}

Talienwan henceforth formed a most convenient base of operations for the attack on Port Arthur, and the siege artillery and line of communications services were landed there instead of at the Hua-yüan river.

Hasegawa's brigade had meantime landed at the latter place on the 1st November and following days, and was {Disembarkation of Hasegawa's Brigade.}

---

* 1st brigade, 1st and 15th regiments; 2nd brigade, 2nd and 3rd regiments.

brought forward to Chinchou after awaiting the landing of the siege artillery from Japan, on the 13th.

Advance of Japanese from Chinchou in two main columns.
The army remained in the neighbourhood of Talienwan and Chinchou till the 17th November, when the advance was continued in two columns.

The right column, consisting of the greater part of the army, advanced by the main road which keeps near the northern shore of the peninsula as far as Tuchêngtzŭ and then turns due south to Port Arthur.

The left column,* formed from part of Hasagawa's brigade, advanced by a road which runs through the centre of the peninsula direct to Port Arthur, but a small force was detached from this column and followed the southern coast road.

Skirmish near Shuangtaikou.
On the 18th November a squadron of cavalry, marching in advance of the 1st Division, found itself unexpectedly engaged with a large Chinese force between Shuangtaikou and Tuchêngtzŭ, and was in imminent danger of being annihilated. The troopers however dismounted and managed to hold their own till relieved by a company of infantry; and the infantry in their turn were hard pressed till further reinforcements arrived, and the Chinese were driven back.

The Japanese lost on this occasion 12 killed and 33 wounded, and the Chinese reported the affair as a great victory, bringing several prisoners into Port Arthur, who were afterwards decapitated.

Japanese advance from Shuangtaikou in three main columns.
At Shuangtaikou that part of Hasegawa's brigade which belonged to the right column and was following the 1st Division, turned off the road and advanced on the left of the 1st Division instead of in rear of it, so that there were now practically three columns instead of two, the 1st Division on the right, main part of Hasegawa's brigade in the centre, and the rest of Hasegawa's brigade on the left.

Japanese positions on 19th November.
On the 19th November Marshal Oyama reached Tuchêngtzŭ. About halfway between this place and the land defences of Port Arthur the main road passes through a range of hills, whilst a branch road skirts their western

---

* This consisted of 2 infantry battalions, a troop of cavalry, a mountain battery, 2 sections of an engineer company, half a bearer company, and half a supply column.

end. The 1st Division was on this branch road, and Hasegawa's Brigade partly on the main road and partly to the east of it, both columns just north of the hills.

The Chinese had an advanced party holding the large village of Shuishiying, which was on the main road between the hills and the Port Arthur defences.

Chinese defensive arrangements at Port Arthur.

The land defences of Port Arthur formed a rough semi-circle of 2½ miles radius, measured from the dockyard. The extreme left of this semicircle was on the western slope of Itzushan Hill, north-west of the dockyard, and the extreme right was the most eastern coast fort. A continuous line of parapets and forts ran along the crests of the hills from one extremity to another, except north of the dockyard, where there is a gap in the hills and the line of defence was broken.

The land forts were armed with a great variety of ordnance, jumbled together in extraordinary confusion, including Krupp, mountain, field, and siege guns, 8-inch mortars, 40-pounder Armstrongs, 10-barrelled Gatlings, and other pieces of ancient pattern.

The main road from Tuchêngtzŭ and Shuishiying passes through this gap. There were three forts on Itzushan Hill, named, in order from the west, Itzushan, Antzushan, and Wangtai, and the next two forts east of the main road were named Sungshushan and Erhlungshan.

From Itzushan to Sungshushan inclusive the forts were garrisoned by 1,650 men, and the next three forts to the east (Erhlungshan and two others) were also garrisoned by 1,650 men. From this section to the extreme right of the position 2,050 men were told off for the defence. In support of this front line there were 1,200 men encamped close in rear of Sungshushan, and 2,550 on the eastern spurs of Cairn Hill, north of the dockyard.

There were 4,050 men manning the coast forts, and about 900 others, chiefly recruits, quartered in and around the dockyard, bringing the total up to 14,050 men. Of these the 1,200 men in rear of Sungshushan and the 2,050 manning the right section of the land defences were fugitives from Talienwan and Chinchou.

On the 20th November Marshal Oyama issued orders for the attack to be made at daylight on the 21st. The 1st Division was to capture the Itzushan forts first, and then co-operate with Hasegawa's brigade in capturing

Orders for attack.

Sungshushan, Erhlungshan, and the others east of the main road.

Chinese sortie. Just as these orders had been issued, about 1 p.m., a force of about 5,000 Chinese advanced through the gap before mentioned to attack the Japanese right, but they were received by shrapnel fire from the Japanese guns and were easily repulsed.

Japanese positions at 6.50 a.m. 21st November. Long before daylight on the 21st November the Japanese troops were on the move, and at 6.50 a.m. they had reached the following positions, apparently unobserved, and certainly unopposed:—

2nd brigade and 2 mountain batteries of 1st Division, 2,500 yards west-north-west of Fort Itzushan.

1st brigade, in support of 2nd brigade.

4 field batteries of 1st Division, supported by 2 battalions of the 1st brigade, on a comparatively low ridge about 3,500 yards north of Fort Itzushan.

The siege artillery, on a low ridge 1,200 yards north of Shuishiying.

Hasegawa's brigade—2 battalions on the ridge east of Shuishiying; 1 battalion and 1 mountain battery on the ridge in rear, east of the main road.

Left column, $2\frac{1}{2}$ miles south-east of the main body of Hasegawa's brigade.

Marshal Oyama, with 1 infantry battalion and a troop of cavalry, stationed himself on the ridge in rear of the siege artillery, west of the main road.

The infantry of the 1st Division had made a difficult march in the dark over an unknown country west of the hills, before arriving at their positions, and the siege artillery had worked unceasingly day and night since the 18th November in order to place their guns in position by dawn of the 21st.

Capture of forts on Itzushan Hill. The battle began by an artillery duel, which lasted from 6.50 a.m. till 8 a.m., the Japanese guns concentrating their fire on the forts on Itzushan Hill.

At 8 a.m. the 2nd infantry brigade was approaching Fort Itzushan from the south-west, and five minutes later the fort was carried with a rush. The Japanese, who were practically unopposed at close quarters, then went straight on up the hill, and at 8.10 a.m. loud cheers announced the capture of all three forts.

Advance of The 1st brigade, which had remained in support, was

PORT ARTHUR CAMPAIGN. 43

then called upon to drive back a Chinese force which was threatening the right flank of the Japanese from the hills west of the harbour. This was accomplished without difficulty, and the two brigades gradually advanced to the Chinese parade ground, south of the gap, and to Cairn Hill, but were unable to proceed further owing to the fire of the coast forts, especially that of Huangchinshan, the fort immediately east of the harbour entrance. *1st Division to parade ground.*

At 8.30 a.m. Hasegawa, seeing that the forts on Itzushan were taken, made preparations for attacking the forts allotted to him, directing his force towards Erhlungshan. *Capture of eastern land forts.*

His men advanced under a heavy fire, but with few casualties, and reached the foot of the hills on which the forts stood at 10.30 a.m., where they rested under cover.

About this time the field artillery of the 1st Division, seeing Hasegawa's brigade advancing, changed position and opened fire against Fort Sungshushan so as to assist in the attack. Hasegawa's men had now to climb a slope of 10° to reach the forts, which were some 300 feet above them, but they moved forward in splendid style, and the Chinese refused to await their onset.

At 11.10 a.m. Sungshushan was evacuated and blown up, and at 11.25 a.m. Erhlungshan also fell, and after this the Chinese made no further stand, but evacuated all the forts east of the main road and harbour, the Japanese left column occupying the line of works from Erhlungshan to the sea with very little fighting.

The Japanese were not prepared to find that Huanchinshan would be given up without a struggle, and spent some time in bringing up their field guns to the east of Cairn Hill and preparing for an attack on this fort.

About 3 p.m., however, it was seen that the fort was abandoned, and nothing remained for the Japanese but to enter the town and take possession. *Occupation of the town.*

The coast forts west of the harbour entrance continued firing for some time at the Japanese fleet, which was slowly steaming past, at a very long range, without replying; but these forts were evacuated during the night. *Western coast forts continued firing, but evacuated during night.*

The Japanese fleet had taken a very small part in the operations. It had been arranged that it should not open fire on the forts during the land attack on account of the risk to the Japanese soldiers, but a few ships went round *Operations of Japanese fleet.*

to Pigeon Bay and headed off some of the fugitives, and the presence of the fleet prevented the Chinese from escaping in steamboats and junks.

Losses. The Japanese lost 66 killed, 353 wounded, and 8 missing.

The Chinese losses were computed at 2,000 killed and a few wounded. The greater part of the garrison escaped along the shore to the east, and so back past Chinchou.

Movements of General Sung. [1] General Sung, as already stated, hearing that the Japanese were marching on Port Arthur, left Haicheng on the 10th November with 2,000 men, and marched south to attack them. It was known that only a small Japanese garrison was left in Chinchou, and Sung hoped at least to be able to recapture that place and cut the Japanese army from its base at Talienwan.

He was joined at Hsiungyao by 6,500 men who had left Yingtzu on 25th October to reinforce Port Arthur, but were too late, and had therefore remained at Hsiungyao.

This reinforcement had brought his strength up to 8,500, and with this force he continued his march southwards, arriving in the vicinity of Chinchou on the 21st November.

Japanese preparations at Chinchou. The Japanese at Chinchou, numbering about 1,500 men, had heard of Sung's approach and had made such preparations as they could to receive him, taking up positions outside the town to the north and north-east.

Sung's attack on Chinchou. On the 21st November Sung attacked, but was driven back with considerable loss, and on the 22nd the fugitives from Port Arthur came crowding past Chinchou and were many of them shot down.

Japanese positions at end of campaign. This ended the Port Arthur campaign. Marshal Oyama with the headquarters of the 1st Division and the 2nd brigade returned to Chinchou; the 1st brigade went north as far as Fuchou, and Hasegawa's brigade remained at Port Arthur.

First peace mission from China. The capture of Port Arthur after a few hours' fighting gave the first real blow to the Peking Government. They now began to realise their military weakness, and the danger they were in; and Mr. Detring, the Commissioner of Customs at Tientsin, was therefore sent to Japan to try and negotiate terms of peace. He arrived, however, without proper credentials, and the Japanese, strongly objecting not only to the manner in which he was sent, but also to the fact of a foreigner being employed on such a mission, refused to treat with him in any way.

---

[1] Captain Cavendish.

CHAPTER V.

EVENTS IN MANCHURIA TILL THE END OF JANUARY, 1895.(¹)

It will be convenient to now resume the narrative of events in Manchuria.

After the capture of Port Arthur, Marshal Yamagata (who was shortly afterwards invalided and succeeded by General Nodzu) received orders to capture Haicheng.

The object of this movement is not very clear: at the commencement of the war the question of an advance on Mukden had been much discussed in Japan, but it is unlikely that this was ever seriously contemplated by the military authorities.

Advance of 3rd Division and capture of Hsi-muchêng and Haicheng.

During the winter months, *i.e.*, from the end of December till the end of February, the coast of Chihli is either ice-bound or weather-bound (the rough weather frequently breaking up the ice), and it appears to have been from the first the intention of the Japanese to postpone the final advance to Peking, which was their ultimate objective, till the early spring, when a landing in Chihli could be safely effected and the Peiho would be navigable.

It was, however, considered necessary for other reasons that something should be done during the winter, and pending the completion of the arrangements for the attack on Weihaiwei* it was probably thought that an advance on Haicheng would serve the most useful purpose by helping to foster the idea of a contemplated attack on Mukden, and thus drawing large numbers of Chinese soldiery from Chihli into Manchuria. Against a more enterprising enemy it would have been a very risky operation, and it undoubtedly entailed great hardships on the Japanese soldier.

On the 3rd December the 3rd Division left Antung for Haichêng.

Its line of advance was by Hsiu-yen and Hsi-muchêng, protected on its right by Tachimi's brigade at Fenghuang-cheng, and to a certain extent on its left by the 1st brigade under General Nogi at Fuchou.†

---

* See Chapter VI.   † See p. 47.
(¹) Japanese official reports: Captain Cavendish, Capain Bower.

On the 8th December most of the Division was concentrated at Hsiu-yen, and on the following day it moved forward towards Hsi-muchêng in three columns.

The right column, under General Oseko, went north to Huang-hua-tien and thence westward towards Hsi-muchêng.

The left column, under Colonel Sato, advanced by a westerly road so as to protect the left flank of the Division against any attack from the direction of Kaiping, where it was known that General Sung had collected a large force.

The centre or main column moved along the main road, starting on the 10th December, one day later than the flank columns.

After a few skirmishes Hsi-muchêng was occupied by the Japanese on the 12th December, and the advance was continued by the right and main columns towards Haicheng.

Colonel Sato's column went westwards as far as Shihmienling, and there remained watching the Chinese forces in the neighbourhood of Kaiping.

On the 13th December the 3rd Division occupied Haicheng without difficulty, the Chinese, who numbered about 7,000, retreating before them to the north-east and north-west, and being practically dispersed.

Operations north and north-east of Fenghuang-chêng.

Whilst this advance of the 3rd Division was being carried out, Tachimi was not idle. He had received orders on the 6th December to make a demonstration so as to divert the attention of the Chinese from the movements of the 3rd Division, and accordingly on 9th December he marched out of Fenghuangchêng, and advanced towards Tsao-ho-kou with about 3,000 men.

At this time the Tatar General I-ko-teng-a (from the northern province of Manchuria) was advancing with 10,000 men to recapture Fenghuangchêng. He himself after communicating with General Nieh-ssŭ-chêng at Motienling, left that place on 6th December and moved down the main road towards Fenghuangchêng with 3,000 men, whilst the rest of his force advanced by the road from Tsaimasui.

On 10th December I and Tachimi met at Pan-chia-tai, and I was driven back with the loss of 110 men killed The Japanese, who had 11 killed and 49 wounded, advanced to Tung-yuan-pu and there halted.

On 11th December a reconnoitring party sent out by

the officer left in command at Fenghuangchêng discovered considerable Chinese forces advancing from Tsaimasui.

Preparations were at once made by the garrison at Fenghuangchêng to resist an attack, and on the 12th the Chinese appeared in the neighbourhood.

They made several unsuccessful attempts to cross the river about 1½ miles east of the town on the 12th and 13th, and on the 14th the Japanese, reinforced by a battalion which had been moved up from Tangshan, assumed the offensive and defeated the Chinese with considerable loss, pursuing them for some distance towards Tsaimasui.

Tachimi, hearing of this attack, sent a part of his force from Tung-yuan-pu across to the Tsaimasui road to attack the enemy's rear, but this detachment arrived only in time to accelerate the Chinese retreat.

After these defeats General I retired to Liaoyang, and, giving up any further attempt against Fenghuangchêng, directed his attention to the recapture of Haicheng.

General Katsura, commanding the Japanese 3rd Division, on arrival at Haicheng, at once began to make preparations for resisting any attack, and occupied for this purpose a semicircle of isolated hills which rise out of the plain to the west, north and east of Haicheng. At the same time he sent spies in all directions in order to learn as much as he could of the strength and movements of the Chinese. *General Katsura at Haicheng.*

The latter were at this time distributed roughly as follows:— *Distribution of Chinese troops.*

Near Kaiping, under General Sung—
  The force defeated at Chinchou, November 21st .. .. .. 8,000 under Sung himself.
  The force defeated at Port Arthur, November 21st .. .. 8,000 „ Hsü-pang-tao.
  Reinforcements from Shantung, sent by way of Yingtzŭ .. 4,000 under Chang.
  At Tashihchiao, reinforcements .. 5,500 „ Liu-chêng-hsiu.

  Total under Sung 25,500

At Tienchuangtai, reinforcements for Sung	6,000
,, Niuchwang, fugitives from Haicheng	2,500
,, Anshanchan, ,, ,,	4,500
,, Motienling, under Nieh-ssŭ-chêng	5,000
,, Liaoyang, under Chang-shun (Kirin troops)	10,000
Under I-ko-teng-a, between Motienling and Liaoyang	10,000
At Mukden, freshly raised troops	15,000

General Sung's movement from Kaiping towards Haicheng.

The Japanese by capturing Haicheng cut the line of communication between Kaiping and Liaoyang, and it was no doubt with the view of preventing this, if possible, that General Sung moved from Kaiping to Tashihchiao on the 12th December with about 9,000 men,* leaving Generals Chang and Hsü near Kaiping with 4,000 and 8,000 men respectively.

Haicheng fell on the 13th December, and this necessitated an alteration of Sung's plans. He could no longer preserve his direct line of communication through Haicheng, and therefore decided to move northwards to Niuchwang, which would give him another line of communication.

General Katsura's movements to intercept Sung.

On the 17th December General Katsura heard of Sung's departure from Kaiping, but as there was no sign of a Chinese army advancing directly towards Haicheng, he drew the conclusion that Sung was moving northwards, and determined to attack him as soon as possible, so as to prevent any chance of his junction with the forces on the Liaoyang road.†

With this object he started from Haicheng before daybreak on the 19th December, and marched westward in search of the Chinese.

Part of the Chinese force had appeared about 3 miles west of Haicheng on the 18th, but had disappeared again by the morning of the 19th, and it was not till 1 p.m. on that day that the 5th Brigade came up with it near the village of Kangwangtsai.

Battle of Kangwangtsai.

As the Chinese were then retreating, the commander of the 5th brigade determined to attack, and soon found himself seriously engaged with a large hostile force.

---

* Joining Liu with his 5,500 men at Tashihchiao.
† See p. 47.

General Katsura had ordered the 6th brigade to return to Haicheng; and that brigade was well on its way homewards when the news reached it that the 5th brigade was engaged with the enemy. It immediately turned westward again and made the best of its way through the snow to join in the fight, but only arrived late in the evening.

The 5th brigade finding itself too weak to turn the Chinese out of the villages in which they had entrenched themselves, waited for the arrival of the 6th brigade; and then after a determined fight, in which they had to make several bayonet charges, the Japanese were finally victorious, driving the Chinese away to the west.

Darkness came on just as the battle ended, but General Katsura nevertheless ordered his men to return at once to Haicheng, leaving only a small party at Kangwangtsai to observe the enemy and guard the wounded.

It was a very hard day's work for the Japanese.

They had started about 2 a.m. on the 19th, and some of them did not reach their quarters again till 2 p.m. on the 20th, after incessant marching through snow 2 feet deep.

The Japanese lost 69 killed and 274 wounded, and the Chinese killed were estimated at 300.

This victory was of great importance for the Japanese, as it not only prevented a junction of Sung's army with that on the Liaoyang road, but also removed all danger of an attack on Haicheng from the west for some time to come, and left the 3rd Division in peace for nearly a month. *Result of battle.*

But though unwilling to attack, the Chinese still remained in strong force to the west. *Chinese still in force west of Haicheng.*

General Ma-yü-kun took command of the reinforcements at Tienchuangtai and brought them forward to the line Niuchang—Yingtzŭ; and Sung, falling back to Tienchuangtai, reorganized his troops behind those of Ma, and was further reinforced on 4th January by 8,000 men from North Chinchou.*

General Chang also remained at Kaiping with 4,000 men.

In these circumstances it was considered advisable at *1st Brigade moved north from Fuchou.*

---

* On the road between Shanhaikuan and Yingtzŭ.

the Japanese headquarters to send a mixed brigade of the 2nd Army northwards from Chinchou to co-operate with the 1st Army.

General Nogi with the 1st brigade was already at Fuchou, and 2 field batteries and 2 squadrons left Chinchou on 1st January to join him.

General Nogi's orders were to capture Kaiping and place himself in communication with the commander of the 1st Army with a view to carrying out his wishes as far as possible, but he remained nominally under the command of Marshal Oyama.

The mixed brigade thus formed then proceeded northwards, reaching Hsiungyao on the 8th January, and arriving within 8 miles of Kaiping on the 9th.

Capture of Kaiping.

On the 10th January at daylight Nogi attacked.

The Chinese were posted between the southern wall of Kaiping and the river, which flows past from east to west at a distance of 250 yards.

They had constructed a rough parapet about 2,000 yards long, and behind this they awaited the attack of the Japanese, who had to cross the frozen river—from 50 to 75 yards of broken ice—before coming to close quarters.

No serious impression was made by the Japanese up till 9.30 a.m., but at that time their scouts reported that a large force was moving up to reinforce the Chinese, and orders were therefore given to attack vigorously, so as to carry the position before the arrival of the new troops.

The Japanese then moved forward over the river and charged across the open space to the parapet, and the Chinese, keeping up a heavy fire till their opponents were about a hundred yards distant, turned and fled towards Yingtzŭ. The force coming up to their assistance from the north halted when the fugitives appeared over the hills, and then returned by the way it came.

This force consisted of the troops under General Hsü's command. He had been ordered to Newchwang shortly after Sung left Kaiping, but when news arrived of the advance of Nogi's brigade he was sent back again to Kaiping to rejoin Chang.

The Japanese losses were 46 killed and 263 wounded, and, according to the report of a Chinese officer, the Chinese had 900 killed and 300 wounded.

The Chinese took up their position to the north-west of Tapingshan, covering Yingtzŭ.

General Nogi established his advance guard at Pei-yun- chai, just over the hills north of Kaiping, in the plain which stretches to Yingtzŭ and Niuchwang; and on the same day he was able to communicate with a battalion of the 3rd Division which had just arrived at Tashihchiao. *Communication between 1st and 2nd Armies.*

It should be mentioned that the Japanese military telegraph line between Chinchou and Takushan, which was begun soon after the landing of the 2nd Army, was completed on 30th December. Takushan was connected with Haicheng by a military line, and Chinchou was connected with Kaiping by an existing Chinese line, so that General Nogi was in communication by telegraph with the 1st Army from the time he left Fuchou.

On the 17th January the Japanese defending Haicheng were attacked by about 15,000 men under Generals I-ko-teng-a of Tsitsihar, Chang-shun of Kirin, and Han-pien-wai of Mongolia. These Tartar and Mongolian forces had been gradually collected at Liaoyang, and moving down the road towards Haicheng they had turned off to the west and extended across country from that road to the Niuchwang-Haicheng road. They then made a convergent attack on Haicheng from the north, but it was most feebly conducted, and was repulsed with ludicrous ease, the Japanese losing 3 killed and 38 wounded, and the Chinese about 300 killed. *First Chinese attack on Haicheng.*

On 22nd January a second attack was made in a similar manner by about 12,000 men, and at the same time about 8,000 under Hsü also advanced from the west. On this occasion the Japanese General tried to draw them on to close quarters, but he was only partially successful in this, and they were driven back with a loss of only 120 killed. *Second attack on Haicheng.*

There were no more attacks till the 16th February, and in the meantime other important events were occurring in the south.

CHAPTER VI.

Wei-hai wei Campaign.

Japanese plans.

After the capture of Port Arthur, the Chinese fleet remained passively at Wei-hai-wei, but although it showed no signs of leaving its shelter, its existence constituted a danger to any Japanese expedition across the Gulf of Pechihli.

The Japanese therefore determined to spend some of the time available, before the date of their projected advance towards Peking, in striking a final decisive blow at the Chinese fleet, and for this purpose an expedition was organized to capture Wei-hai-wei.

Employment of Japanese transports after fall of Port Arthur.

The Japanese transports had been engaged for a long time after the fall of Port Arthur in taking supplies from Japan to the different points on the coasts of Korea, Shingking, and the Liaotung peninsula, whence they could most easily be forwarded to the front. These points were Chemulpo, Ping Yang inlet, Kwimpo,* near the mouth of the Yalu south of Wiju, Takushan, and Talienwan. But at the beginning of January a fleet of transports was collected at Ujina and Shimonoseki ready for the new expedition.

Organisation of force for Wei-hai-wei Expedition.

The troops detailed for the expedition† were the 2nd Division and that portion of the 6th Division which had not yet left Japan.‡ They were to be considered as an addition to the 2nd Army, and therefore came under the command of Marshal Oyama.

Rendezvous at Talienwan.

After careful reconnaissance it was decided to disembark the troops at Yungchêng Bay, at the extreme north-east point of the Shantung peninsula, and the whole expedition assembled in Talienwan Bay on the 17th January and following days prior to the disembarkation.

Bombardment of Tungchou.

(²) On the 18th January three cruisers left Talienwan and proceeded to Tungchou, a town west of Chifu, which

---

* Korean pronunciation.

† About 24,000 officers and men, with 48 field and mountain guns, and 12 mortars, and 13,000 coolies and soldiers employed as coolies.

‡ See p. 72.

(¹) Captain Du Boulay.

(²) "The China-Japan War," by Vladimir, p. 270.

they bombarded the same day. The bombardment was continued on the 19th, and the squadron rejoined the rest of the fleet off the Shantung promontory early on the 20th. The object of this bombardment was to divert the attention of the Chinese from the actual point of disembarkation.

(¹) On the 19th January 19 transports, carrying part of the 2nd Division, left Talienwan; 11 more carrying the rest of the Division followed on the 20th; and on the 22nd the headquarters of the army and the troops of the 6th Division left in 20 ships. *(Departure of expedition from Talienwan.)*

(²) The first flotilla, which was escorted by the main and 2nd squadrons of the fleet,* and preceded by the *Yayeyama*, reached Yungchêng Bay at daylight on the 20th January. A body of 300 Chinese with 4 guns was at the landing place and prepared to resist the landing, but a few rounds from the *Yayeyama* dispersed them, and the disembarkation then went on continuously without any hitch till the whole army was landed, together with supplies of food for six weeks. *(Arrival at Yungchêng Bay, and disembarkation.)*

---

* (²) Organisation of Japanese fleet:—

"Main" Squadron—
  Matsushima.
  Itsukushima.
  Hashidate.
  Chiyoda.

1st, "Flying," Squadron—
  Yoshino.
  Akitsushima.
  Naniwa.
  Takachiho.

2nd Squadron—
  Fuso.
  Kongo.
  Hiyei.
  Takao.

3rd Squadron—
  Tsukushi.
  Katsuragi.
  Yamato.
  Musashi.
  Tenriu.

4th Squadron—
  Akagi.
  Maya.
  Oshima.
  Chokai.
  Atago.

Not attached to a squadron—
  4 sloops.

Torpedo boats—
  1st Flotilla—*Kotaka.*
    and Nos. 7, 11, 13, 23.

  2nd Flotilla—
    Nos. 8, 9, 14, 18, 19, 21.

  3rd Flotilla—
    Nos. 5, 6, 10, 22.

(¹) Captain Du Boulay.
(²) Japanese official reports: *Revue Militaire de l'Étranger.*

Yungchêng Bay was admirably suited for a landing place, and without any apparent effort the 2nd Division completed its disembarkation in three days—20th, 21st, and 22nd, and the 6th Division in two days, 23rd and 24th. The Headquarter Staff landed on the 25th and went to Yungchêng, a walled town 8 miles distant, which had been occupied by troops of the 2nd Division in the afternoon of the 20th.

For the first few days after the arrival of the expedition at Yungchêng Bay the main part of the Japanese fleet kept the sea, leaving the lighter vessels to guard the transports, and keeping a close watch on Wei-hai-wei by means of 3 cruisers of the 1st "Flying" Squadron, supplemented at night by 10 torpedo boats. Afterwards when the Chinese fleet showed no signs of coming out, only one squadron at a time went out for 24 hours; but the harbour was always watched by one cruiser by day, and whatever the weather the torpedo boats were always out at night.

Advance from Yungchêng.

From Yungchêng the advance towards Wei-hai-wei was made by two roads.

The 6th Division formed the right column, and advanced by the coast road.

The 2nd Division formed the left column, and advanced by a parallel road about 4 miles inland.

A detachment was left at a town $5\frac{1}{2}$ miles south of Yungchêng to guard the line of communications against any attack from that direction.

The general advance began on the 26th January, but the cavalry and part of the 3rd Brigade had been already sent forward along the inland road to reconnoitre and repair the road where necessary.

Skirmishes took place between this brigade and the Chinese on the 26th and 27th, but the Chinese made no real stand.

Positions of Japanese on 28th January.

(¹) On the 28th the left column reached Chung-chia-kou-tzŭ,* and the right column Pao-chia; and steps were taken to reconnoitre the enemy's position at Wei-hai-wei.

Defences and garrison of Wei-hai-wei.

(¹) The defences of Wei-hai-wei fall naturally into three groups, namely, those on the Islands of Liu-kung-tao and

---

* A detachment was posted on the road to Wentêng, and remained there during the rest of the operations.

(¹) Captain Du Boulay, and Japanese official reports.

WEI-HAI-WEI CAMPAIGN.

I-tao, those on the mainland at the northern or western entrance of the harbour, and those on the mainland at the southern or eastern entrance.

A few small works had also been made to command the main road from Chifu to Wei-hai-wei town.

The ordinary garrison consisted of 2,700 men on the mainland and 1,000 on the islands; but these numbers had been modified on the one hand by the despatch of troops to Asan, and on the other by the arrival of fresh troops from other parts of the Shantung province; and at the time of the Japanese attack the numbers were said to be 1,500 on the islands, 3,000 in the western mainland forts, and 3,000 in the eastern mainland forts.* In addition to these, the Chinese fleet, consisting of 2 battle-ships, 5 cruisers, 1 sloop, 6 gunboats, 1 torpedo gunboat, and 11 torpedo boats, manned by some 4,000 sailors, was lying in the harbour. The two entrances to the harbour were closed by booms, but a small opening was left in each for the passage of one ship at a time. The coast forts were all armed with modern breechloading heavy guns.

On the mainland at the eastern entrance there were five of these forts, named, in succession from the left, Lung-miao-tsui, Lu-chueh-tsui, Chao-pei-tsui, Shai-chia-su, and Yang-fung-ting; the last mentioned commanding Three Peak Bay. These forts were defended against a land attack by a line of parapet running westwards from Yang-fung-ting and reaching the sea coast between Forts Lung-miao-tsui and Lu-chueh-tsui. At the most commanding point of this line of parapet was a small fort named Motienling armed with field guns, and between Motienling and Lu-chueh-tsui was another smaller fort also armed with light guns.

(¹) About 3½ miles south of Yang-fung-ting is a high peak, from which extensive views can be obtained in all directions, and half-way between this peak and the Chinese defences flows a river, which coming from the south-west and winding along at the foot of the peak, after many sharp turns falls into Three Peak Bay. This river was frozen over at the time of the Japanese attack, and was generally fordable even when the ice was broken.

Country between the opposing forces.

---

* About 4,000 men left Tientsin on 24th January to march 600 miles and reinforce Wei-hai-wei, but were naturally too late.

(¹) Captain Du Boulay.

56   AN EPITOME OF THE CHINO-JAPANESE WAR.

Advance of 2nd Division on 29th January.

(¹) On the 29th January, as a preliminary to an attack on the following day, the 2nd Japanese Division, driving in some outlying Chinese troops, advanced to a point on the river north-west of Chung-chia-kou-tzŭ and established its outpost line along the spurs of the hills southwards and eastwards of this point.

The 6th Division continued the outpost line to the sea along a spur which ran in a north-easterly direction from the high peak.

Japanese orders for attack.

(¹) Orders were issued on the 29th January for an attack on the following morning by the 2nd Division, so as to occupy the ridges which separated it from the southern end of the harbour, and which were held by the Chinese.

At the same time the 6th Division was ordered to act as a reserve on the right to guard against a counter attack from the forts.

It is probable however that some further instructions were issued by army headquarters, since the 6th Division was expressly ordered by its commander to attack the hills in its front, instead of merely acting as a reserve.

Commencement of the attack.

(¹) The attacks both on the left and right were begun at 6.50 a.m. on the 30th January; and at the same time six of the light division ships of the Japanese fleet steamed into Three Peak Bay, and began a long range bombardment of the two eastern forts, which continued till 11.30 a.m.

Left attack.

(¹) On the left the 2nd Division had very little difficulty in carrying the successive ridges, and by 9.30 a.m. its work was practically completed; a battalion then pursued the Chinese along the beach to the west, and suffered some loss in consequence from the fire of three or four Chinese vessels which steamed in as close as the shallow water would permit.

Right attack: capture of land defences.

(¹) On the right the attack was in the first instance directed against Motienling; and this fort fell at 8.15 a.m. without much loss to the attackers, in spite of the enfilading fire from Yang-fung-ting. A few minutes later the other small fort near Motienling was also carried, and the land defences were all in the hands of the Japanese.

The Japanese had now to experience a hot fire from the coast forts and the Chinese ships, but they were in a commanding position as regards the former, and were able to bring a heavy fire from their mountain batteries and

---

(¹) Japanese official reports, and Captain Du Boulay.

from the Chinese field guns found in Motienling, against Yang-fung-ting, which was their next objective.

General Odela, commanding the 11th brigade, who was directing operations in Motienling, was killed by a shell during this time.

(¹) At 12.30 p.m. Yang-fung-ting caught fire and was abandoned; Shai-chia-su was evacuated immediately afterwards; and five minutes later an explosion occurred in Chao-pei-tsui, which was also abandoned.

Capture of coast forts.

The garrisons of these forts fled westwards along the shore, and as they crossed the front of the Japanese battalion which had occupied the small fort near Motienling, they suffered very heavy loss.

(²) The Chinese admiral, Ting, foreseeing the loss of the eastern forts, had begun to dismantle them before the arrival of the Japanese, fearing that the heavy guns would be turned against his ships as soon as they were captured. His action in this matter however was not approved, and the guns were again put in proper order in obedience to peremptory orders from Tientsin. When therefore it was seen that the forts were about to fall into the hands of the Japanese, a party of 30 Chinese bluejackets made a bold attempt to land and disable the guns in Lu-chueh-tsui, but it was too late, and both Lu-chueh-tsui and Lung-miao-tsui were abandoned by their garrisons and occupied at 12.45 p.m. by the Japanese.

(¹) The Japanese on their side had also calculated on the probability of being able to utilize the heavy guns in these forts, and a party of bluejackets had accompanied the army for the express purpose of manning them, and had brought sundry stores and fittings from Port Arthur to replace similar articles which would probably be removed or destroyed by the Chinese.

Employment of the heavy guns in the captured forts by the Japanese.

There were four 24-cm. guns in Lu-chueh-tsui ; three of these were made ready for action as soon as possible, and at 1.15 p.m. fire was opened from them against I-tao.

This drew the attention of the Chinese ships and forts, and a heavy fire was concentrated on Lu-chueh-tsui, by which two of the guns were disabled. The Japanese kept up the unequal fight till 4 p.m. and then ceased firing, and the Chinese, supposing that they had withdrawn from the fort, ceased firing also shortly afterwards.

(¹) Japanese official reports, and Captain Du Boulay.
(²) Captain Cavendish.

Results of the fighting on 30th January.

(¹) This ended the day's fighting, which had been highly satisfactory for the Japanese; the whole of the eastern mainland forts were in their hands, they commanded one end of the boom across the eastern entrance, and the submarine mines were rendered innocuous. Their losses were 64 killed and 162 wounded.

Positions for the night.

(¹) For that night the 6th Division remained in the neighbourhood of Shai-chia-su, and the 2nd Division found quarters in the villages between the southern end of the harbour and the river.

31st January.

(¹) The 31st January was passed by the Japanese in making preparations for future movements, and especially in preparing the heavy guns in the captured coast forts for action. It had been arranged that a torpedo boat attack should be made during the night, but a northerly gale sprang up in the afternoon with snow, and the attack was necessarily abandoned.

Movements on 1st February.

(¹) On the following day, 1st February, the 6th Division, leaving a garrison in the eastern forts, closed to its left to take the place of the 2nd Division, which began to move forward towards Wei-hai-wei town. The advance of the latter division was made in a north-westerly direction to the point where the road from Chifu to Wei-hai-wei bends to the north. It was a long detour, and the tracks over the hills were rendered almost impassable in places owing to the storm which continued to rage all day, but the direct road along the coast could not be used as it was commanded by the guns of the Chinese fleet.

Fight on Japanese left.

(¹) A small detachment of the 2nd Division which was acting as a left flank guard, on reaching the Chifu road in a heavy snow storm, found itself unexpectedly in the presence of about 2,500 Chinese, and a sharp fight ensued. The Japanese were in a critical position, but reinforcements quickly arrived, and the Chinese were driven westwards. It afterwards transpired that the Chinese formed part of the garrison of the western mainland forts, and that they were making their escape towards Chifu before their last line of retreat was cut off. They lost about 100 killed, whilst the Japanese lost 6 killed and 39 wounded.

Japanese fleet withdrawn for shelter from storm.

The weather was so bad during the day that the Japanese fleet withdrew to Yungchêng Bay, leaving only the 1st Squadron at Three Peak Bay to keep a watch on the harbour.

(¹) Japanese official reports, and Captain Du Boulay.

WEI-HAI-WEI CAMPAIGN.

(¹) On the 2nd February the 2nd Division entered Wei-hai-wei unopposed, and it was discovered that the western mainland forts had all been abandoned and the guns rendered useless. (²) It appears that Admiral Ting, seeing the soldiers deserting the forts, had sent a party of sailors ashore to disable the guns before they fell into Japanese hands. *Occupation of Wei-hai-wei town.*

The Japanese fleet put to sea again on the 2nd, but according to Admiral Ito's report, "the cold was so intense that the ships were covered with ice, and blocks of ice three to five inches thick were frozen into the muzzles of the guns." *Japanese fleet put to sea again, 2nd February.*

The Japanese Army had now finished the work assigned to it, and it remained for the Navy, with the assistance of the eastern forts, to bring about the reduction of the remaining Chinese defences, namely, the fleet and the forts on Liu-kung-tao and I-tao.

(¹) The weather was fine again on the 3rd February, and a bombardment was kept up for a great part of the day between the ships and forts on both sides, and during the night some Japanese torpedo boats tried to cut the boom in the eastern entrance of the harbour. They were unsuccessful in this, but they discovered that it was possible for boats to pass between the southern end of the boom and the shore, though the passage was extremely difficult owing to the rocks. *Bombardment, 3rd February.*

(¹) In consequence of this discovery, Admiral Ito gave orders for an attack to be made during the night of the 4th–5th February, by the 2nd and 3rd torpedo boat flotillas, consisting respectively of 6 and 4 boats. *First torpedo boat attack.*

The attack was made immediately after the moon set in the early morning of the 5th February.* The 3rd flotilla, which led, passed into the harbour successfully, but the 2nd flotilla got into difficulties, and only 4 boats managed eventually to pass the boom.

It was intended that all the boats should move towards the western shore of the harbour before attacking; but as those of the 2nd flotilla had lost so much time at the boom, they were steered directly from the entrance towards the Chinese ships.

---

* The gunboats *Chokai* and *Atago* had been firing into the harbour for some time before this, so as to divert the attention of the Chinese.

(¹) Japanese official reports, and Captain Du Boulay.
(²) Captain Du Boulay.

The 2nd flotilla was discovered whilst still at the boom by the Chinese guard boats, and a brisk fire was opened, but in the confusion No. 9 boat managed to discharge a torpedo at a two-masted ship believed to be the *Ting-yuen*. The boat however was immediately afterwards hit by a shell from the ship, which pierced the boiler, killing 4 men and wounding 4 others. No. 19 boat came to her assistance, and after taking off the rest of the crew, and towing her to the southern shore, returned to Three Peak Bay. No. 21 likewise came upon No. 8 with a damaged propeller and escorted her out of the harbour.

During the firing the boats of the 3rd flotilla continued their course westwards unnoticed by the Chinese; and on nearing the western shore turned to starboard and steered towards the Chinese fleet. They were discovered before long, and a heavy fire was opened upon them, but they kept steadily advancing and succeeded in discharging six torpedoes when within a range of 400 yards from the ships. It was impossible to tell however whether any hits had been made owing to the smoke and darkness.

On the way out of the harbour No. 22 boat ran on the rocks in front of Lung-miao-tsui and was wrecked.

During the afternoon the *Ting-yuen*, which was the only ship hit by a torpedo, gradually sank in shallow water.

The Japanese lost 19 men and one boat, and two other boats were so badly damaged that they were towed over to Port Arthur for repairs.

Second torpedo boat attack.

(¹) The next night the 1st flotilla, consisting of five boats, was sent into the harbour, whilst the 2nd and 3rd flotillas were sent to the western entrance to make a demonstration and divert the attention of the Chinese.

The boats of the 1st flotilla passed the boom after some little delay, steamed right round the harbour as far as the point south-east of Wei-hai-wei town, and then turned eastwards and advanced to the attack. They were observed as they approached the Chinese ships, but managed to fire seven torpedoes within effective range, and then retire out of the harbour without suffering any loss or damage at all.

At daylight it was seen that the *Lai-yuen* and *Wei-yuen* an the despatch boat *Pashua** had been sunk.

---

* A tug boat used as a despatch boat.
(¹) Japanese official reports, and Captain Du Boulay.

A general bombardment took place on the 7th February, and during the course of it the fort on I-tao island was silenced. One of its disappearing 8-inch guns was disabled by a shot from Fort Lung-miao-tsui, and shortly afterwards one of its cartridge stores was blown up by a shell from Chao-pei-tsui. (¹) *[marginal: Bombardment on 7th February.]*

Whilst the bombardment was proceeding the 11 Chinese torpedo boats left the harbour by the western entrance, and tried to escape westwards, but they were all either sunk or captured. *[marginal: Attempted escape of Chinese torpedo boats.]*

(¹) The absence of these boats enabled the Japanese to place twelve 9-cm. mortars in position near one of the western forts so as to bring an artillery fire to bear on the western end of Liu-kung-tao and also on the Chinese ships, which generally assembled in this neighbourhood beyond the range of the eastern forts. So long as the Chinese torpedo boats were in the harbour they were able to prevent any movements of the Japanese near the western forts by means of their quick-firing and machine gun fire.

On the 9th February another general bombardment took place, and a long range shot from Lu-chueh-tsui hit and sank the Chinese cruiser *Ching-yuen*, whilst the 9-cm. mortars completely silenced the western fort on Liu-kung-tao. (¹) *[marginal: Bombardment on 9th February.]*

There was another bombardment for a short time on the 11th February, and on the 12th Admiral Ting offered to surrender, on condition that the lives of the surviving defenders, both European and Chinese, should be spared. *[marginal: Bombardment on 11th February. Proposal to surrender.]*

(¹) Negotiations followed, and on 16th February the surrender took place, the Japanese fleet entering the harbour on the 17th. *[marginal: Surrender of Chinese.]*

It is difficult to arrive at a correct estimate of the losses of the Chinese on Liu-kung-tao, but they cannot have been very heavy, and were certainly not sufficient to warrant a surrender. It was stated that the "shrapnel caused such loss amongst the garrison that it brought about the surrender;"* but the only shrapnel shells fired by the Japanese were from the 9-cm. mortars on the 9th February, and though these may have inflicted considerable loss on the garrison of the extreme western fort, and possibly also

---

* Statement made to Captain Cavendish. See his Report, 31st March, 1895.

(¹) Japanese official reports, and Captain Du Boulay.

on board the *Chen-yuen*, such loss was only local and should not have affected the whole garrison of Liu-kung-tao.

Effect of bombardment.
(¹) During the several days' bombardment that took place the Japanese ships did practically no damage to *matériel* on Liu-kung-tao, but their principal object was to draw the Chinese fire and divert it from the eastern forts, and they generally therefore kept out at a long range—from 4,000 to 6,000 yards. The ships themselves were occasionally hit, and they had altogether 8 killed and 34 wounded on board.

Chinese ships taken by Japanese.
(¹) The Chinese ships handed over to the Japanese were the *Chen-yuen*, *Tsi-yuen*, *Ping-yuen*, *Kuang-ping*, and six small gunboats. The *Kang-chi* was not taken over, but left in the hands of the Chinese for the purpose of conveying the body of Admiral Ting, who had committed suicide on the 12th, to Chifu.

Of the 11 Chinese torpedo boats which tried to escape on the 7th February, 6 were afterwards repaired and added to the Japanese fleet.

The *Chen-yuen*, which had run aground on entering Wei-hai-wei harbour on the 7th November, was docked at Port Arthur by the Japanese before being taken to Japan.

Withdrawal of Japanese from Wei-hai-wei.
Having captured Wei-hai-wei and completely destroyed the naval power of China, the next step of the Japanese was to concentrate their forces near Talienwan and Port Arthur, and prepare for the final expedition against Peking itself. All the guns therefore on the mainland at Wei-hai-wei were either destroyed or removed, and by the end of February the whole army was withdrawn, except a small garrison in Liu-kung-tao. The 2nd Division was stationed between Talienwan and Port Arthur, and the troops of the 6th Division joined the rest of that Division at Port Arthur itself. (¹)

(¹) Japanese official reports, and Captain Du Boulay.

CHAPTER VII.

EVENTS IN MANCHURIA FROM THE COMMENCEMENT OF FEBRUARY. CONCLUSION OF THE WAR.

(¹) On the 16th February Haicheng was again attacked by the Chinese, some 15,000 men advancing from the north, north-west, and west, under Generals Chang-shun (of Kirin), I-ko-teng-a, and Hsü-pang-tao; but again they were easily repulsed, losing 150 men killed, whilst the Japanese had only 3 killed and 11 wounded. Third attack on Haicheng.

(¹) On the following day the Japanese troops forming the garrison of Hsi-mucheng—one battalion of the 3rd Division and some of the 2nd reserve infantry—were attacked from the east by about 1,000 men, probably local robbers, but drove them off without loss to themselves. Chinese attack on Hsi-mucheng.

(¹) On the 21st February the Chinese again made a demonstration against Haicheng, but nothing was done beyond a little long range artillery firing. Reinforcements had meantime arrived on both sides in the direction of Yingtzŭ. Fourth attack on Haicheng. Arrival of additional troops on both sides.

(²) On the Chinese* side General Wutachêng, with 10,000 men had reached Tienchuangtai from Shanhaikuan on the 6th February; and on the Japanese side the remainder of the 1st Division under General Yamaji had moved up from Chinchou to Kaiping.† This force left Chinchou on the 10th February and following days, and began to arrive at Kaiping on the 20th.

(³) On that day the outposts of the 2nd brigade, which had hitherto been stretched across the plain 9 miles north of Kaiping, were pushed forward another 3 miles to Tapingshan Hill. This is a remarkable hill about 2 miles long and 180 feet high, standing by itself in the middle of the plain, and therefore of considerable military importance. Occupation of Tapingshun by Japanese outposts.

(³) On the 21st February, however, General Ma-yü-kun, with part of Sung's army, drove back the Japanese outposts and occupied the hill. Japanese outposts driven back from Tapingshan.

---

* General Chang, with the remnants of his Shantung brigade, left Yingtzŭ on 9th February to march to the Shantung province and guard the road from Wei-hai-wei to Peking.

† The 1st Division was from this time transferred from the 2nd Army to the 1st Army.

(¹) Japanese official reports.
(²) ,, ,, and Captain Cavendish.
(³) ,, ,, ,, Du Boulay.

Battle of Tapingshan, and its re-occupation by Japanese.

(¹) General Yamaji, recognising the importance of having Tapingshan in his possession, determined to recapture it as soon as the 1st Division was collected north of Kaiping. This was effected on the 23rd February, and at daylight on the 24th the attack was made.

The Chinese were soon driven from the hill itself, but they remained massed in the villages immediately to the north of it, and General Yamaji, who was unwilling to advance beyond the hill, tried the effect of an artillery bombardment to drive them out. This, however, failed, and eventually the infantry were sent forward, upon which the Chinese retreated all along the line.

The Japanese lost 30 killed and 220 wounded, and no less than 1,500 men suffered from frostbite. There were two feet of snow on the ground, and the thermometer registered zero Fahrenheit.

The Chinese losses are not known, but 800 wounded were afterwards treated in the Red Cross Hospital which had been established by the Europeans and Americans at Yingtzŭ.

Japanese plans.

The objective of the Japanese in Manchuria was now Yingtzŭ, which they proposed to make use of as a post for landing stores, &c., as soon as the ice in the Liao river should break up. But on the one hand it was considered that the 1st Division was not strong enough of itself to ensure the capture of the place, and on the other hand the 3rd Division could hardly be moved in that direction as long as there were large hostile forces to the north and north-east of Haicheng.*

---

* The Chinese forces were estimated as follows:—

On road to Liaoyang—
  Under I .. .. 20 camps.
  „ Chang-shun .. .. .. 20 „
Niuchwang—
  Under Hsü-pang-tao .. .. .. 13 „
  „ Wei-kuang-shou .. .. .. 6 „
  „ Liu-shu-yüan .. .. .. 4 „
Yingtzŭ and vicinity—
  Under Sung .. .. 52 „
Motienling—
  Under Nieh .. .. 10 „

          Total .. .. .. 125 camps.
          or 62,500 men.

(¹) Japanese official reports, and Captain Du Boulay.

General Nodzu accordingly decided that the 1st Division should remain stationary, whilst the 3rd Division should march out of Haicheng and, assisted by part of the 5th Division, should defeat the enemy on the Liaoyang road.

The 3rd and 5th Divisions should then turn westwards by way of Niuchwang towards Yingtzŭ, where they would be joined by the 1st Division for a combined movement against Sung's forces. The 1st Division was to send a small force to Haicheng to assist in its defence during the early part of this programme.

(¹) On the 21st February the troops of the 5th Division who were to take part in these operations, about 6,000 men with 24 guns, left Fenghuangchêng. Their route lay by Huanghuatien, and thence by a mountain road to Anshanchan, which they were timed to reach on 2nd March. Departure of troops of 5th Division from Fenghuangchêng for Anshanchan.

(¹) The 3rd Division completed its preparations by the 27th February, and marched out of Haicheng at 4 a.m. on the 28th. The Chinese were in considerable force to the north, and the first move was therefore made in that direction. About 5.30 a.m. the first Chinese position, on a hill 2½ miles north of Haicheng, was carried, and the Chinese were then gradually driven back to the north and north-west. 3rd Division leaves Haicheng for Anshanchan.

As soon as this was effected the Japanese made a general move eastwards so as to gain the Liaoyang road, keeping the greater part of the 5th brigade, under General Oseko, as a detached force to guard their left flank, whilst two battalions remained north-west of Haicheng to watch the country in that direction. These two battalions returned to Haicheng on the following day, and formed, with the troops sent from the 1st Division, the garrison for the time being.

(¹) The Japanese lost during the day 15 killed and 109 wounded, and the Chinese over 400 killed. The Chinese had apparently intended to make another attack on Haicheng on the 28th February, for whilst the Japanese were marching out to the north-east, about 2,500 Chinese under General Hsü-pang-tao advanced against the western defences. They were met, however, by the troops of the 1st Division, and driven back again without any difficulty. Fifth attack on Haicheng.

(¹) Japanese official reports.

Advance of 3rd Division towards Anshanchan.

The main body of the 3rd Division halted in the neighbourhood of Tóu-ho-pou for the night, and on the 1st March the advance was resumed along the Liaoyang road.

(¹) The Chinese, to the number of 4,000, were posted at Chien-hsien-pu, but finding themselves threatened in front by the main body of the 3rd Division, and on their left flank by a battalion which had marched across country from Hsi-muchêng, they hurriedly retreated, and took up a position on a hill about two miles to the north.

On the 2nd March it was arranged that General Oseko's detached force should attack the right of the Chinese, whilst the main body should attack their front; but it was found that they had abandoned their position during the night, and the advance of the Japanese was therefore continued to Anshanchan. It was expected that the Chinese would make a stand here, but again they retreated without fighting, no doubt alarmed by the arrival of the troops of the 5th Division on their left flank. (¹) The latter had suffered much from the cold during their difficult march through the hills, but had had no fighting beyond a few very slight skirmishes.

Arrival at Anshanchan of 3rd and 5th Divisions.

Advance of 3rd and 5th Divisions towards Niuchwang.

(¹) A detachment was left at Anshanchan, and the two Japanese divisions then turned westwards and marched about 3½ miles towards Niuchwang, the 3rd Division halting at Chiang-chia-tun, with the 5th Division to its left rear.

Sixth attack on Haicheng.

(¹) During this day, the 2nd March, about 1,500 Chinese under Hsü-pang-tao advanced from the direction of Niuchwang towards Haicheng, probably thinking that there were no Japanese left to defend it; but they soon found out their mistake, and retired at once.

Capture of Niuchwang.

(¹) On 3rd March the Japanese army halted about 6½ miles east of Niuchwang, and orders were issued for an attack to be made on that place on the following day.

Niuchwang was held by 5,000 Hunanese "braves" who had been sent forward from Peking about the end of December,(²) but on the approach of the Japanese, on the 4th March, about 2,000 of them departed towards Kaokán, leaving the place to be defended by the remaining 3,000.

The Japanese 3rd Division moved round and attacked the town from the north and west, whilst the 5th Division attacked from the east and south. The first houses were

---

(¹) Japanese official reports.
(²) Captain Cavendish.

CONCLUSION OF THE WAR. 67

reached about noon, after firing had been going on for two hours, and from that time onwards the struggle was a severe one.

The Chinese made a determined resistance in the houses, and until 5 p.m. no very great success was achieved by the Japanese. After that however a more systematic method of attack was adopted, and each house or block of houses was reduced in succession, guns being brought forward in some cases to knock down the walls.

In this way the Chinese were gradually subdued, some of them fighting to the last, and others surrendering when they saw that further resistance was hopeless, and at 11 p.m. firing ceased.

The Japanese lost in this fight 70 killed and 319 wounded; and of the 3,000 Chinese about 2,000 were killed and 633 made prisoners.

([1]) On the same day General Wutachêng arrived at Yingtzŭ from Tienchuangtai, but without his troops, and on the other hand General Sung, anticipating the advance of the Japanese, began to move his army back towards Tienchuangtai, vacating his position between Tapingshan and Yingtzŭ, which was at once occupied by the Japanese 1st Division. *Retreat of Sung to Tienchuangtai, and advance of 1st Division.*

([2]) On the 5th March the 3rd and 5th Divisions leaving one battalion to garrison Niuchwang, marched 7 miles towards Yingtzŭ; and on the same day the troops sent from the 1st Division to Haicheng rejoined their Division. *Advance of 3rd and 5th Divisions continued.*

([2]) On the 6th the three Japanese Divisions advanced to the line Yingtzŭ-Kaokán, 3rd Division on the right, 5th Division in the centre, and 1st Division on the left. Part of the 1st Division occupied the town of Yingtzŭ; but the forts at the mouth of the river did not change hands till the following morning. *Occupation of Yingtzŭ.*

A heavy snow storm on the 7th March prevented the Japanese from carrying out a reconnaisance in force which was arranged for that day, but a small detachment advanced to within 3 miles of Tienchuangtai, driving in a Chinese outpost. *Advance of three Japanese divisions towards Tienchuangtai.*

([2]) On the 8th March the Japanese Divisions once more moved forward. The 3rd Division advanced by the

---

([1]) Japanese official reports, and Captain Cavendish.
([2])   ,,   ,,

Kaókán Tienchuangtai road to the point where it is joined by the road from Yingtzŭ; the 1st Division moved along the latter road and halted to the left rear of the 3rd Division, and the 5th Division crossed the route of the 3rd Division and moved up to its right. A reconnaissance in force under General Oshima (commanding 6th brigade) showed that the Chinese had over 30 guns in position along the river front of Tienchuangtai. Their strength was probably about 30,000 men, of whom 20,000 belonged to Sung's army, and 10,000 had come up from Shanhaikuan with Wutachêng. Wutachêng himself, it appears, did not remain for the fighting, and was afterwards " disgraced."

Battle of Tienchuangtai.

([1]) The Japanese attacked at 7.30 a.m. on the 9th March. They massed all their artillery—91 guns—on the left bank of the river, opposite Tienchuangtai, supported by the 1st brigade on the left and the 3rd Division on the right, and sent the 2nd brigade by a detour round the Chinese right flank, and the 5th Division round their left flank.

From 9.30 a.m. till 10 a.m. fighting was going on at the south end of Tienchuangtai (*i.e.*, the Chinese right), along its river front, and also about 4,000 yards above the town where the 5th Division crossed the river and found itself opposed by 3,000 Chinese.

At 10 a.m. the 5th Division succeeded in dispersing this force and then advanced towards the north end of Tienchuangtai. The Chinese made no vigorous stand after this, but tried to escape to the north-west, west, and south-west.

A large number succeeded, but many were shot down as they crossed the front of the 1st and 5th Divisions.

At 11 a.m. the town was in flames, and the Japanese who had entered it were withdrawn.

The Japanese had 16 killed and 144 wounded, and the Chinese killed were estimated at 2,000.

Movements after Tienchuangtai.

([1]) The Chinese retreated to North Chinchou, and the country was now clear of them on both banks of the Liao river for a distance of 30 to 40 miles north-east of Yingtzŭ, whilst on the Liaoyang road their most advanced post was north-east of Anchanchan.

With a view to interfering as little as possible with the Treaty Port of Yingtzu,* and in order to shorten the main

---

([1]) Japanese official reports.
* Commonly called Niuchuang.

CONCLUSION OF THE WAR.

lines of communication as much as possible, the following dispositions were now made by the Japanese: the 1st Division retired to Kaiping; the 3rd Division to Kangwangtsai, with detachments at Yingtzŭ and Niuchwang; and the 5th Division to Haicheng, with a detachment at Anshanchan. The brigade under General Tachimi still held Fenghuangchêng and the road thence to Chiulienchêng, and a few small skirmishes occurred between portions of this brigade and Chinese local forces in the hills north-east of Chiulienchêng; but the war was now practically over, and the Chinese were making a *bonâ fide* attempt to obtain peace.

Mr. Detring, as already mentioned, was sent to Japan after the fall of Port Arthur, but his mission failed, and the Chinese Government then decided to send two envoys to treat for peace. The men selected were Chang-yu-yuan and Shao-yu-lien, and the services of Mr. Foster, an American, were obtained to assist them. *Peace negotiations. Second mission.*

They had to wait for Mr. Foster's arrival, and even then delayed their departure from Shanghai for some time, and, finally, only reached Japan on the 30th January, the day on which the eastern defences of Wei-hai-wei were captured.

This mission fell through at once, as it was found that the envoys had been sent without proper credentials, and had not received full powers to settle the terms of peace.

The Chinese Government proposed to amend the credentials, but this was not agreed to by the Japanese, and eventually they determined to send the Viceroy Li-Hung-Chang, to Japan. He was the only man in China of sufficient authority and knowledge to undertake the negotiations, and was probably the only man whom the Japanese would have accepted as an envoy. *Third mission.*

Li-Hung-Chang, accompanied by his son, "Lord" Li, landed at Shimonoseki on 20th March, where he was met by Count Ito, the Japanese plenipotentiary, and negotiations were at once opened.

(¹) But shortly before this a force of 4,500 men from the 2nd Reserves had left Japan in five transports, accompanied by men-of-war, and on the 21st March they landed *Japanese expedition to the Pescadores.*

(¹) Captain Du Boulay.

on Fisher Island in the Pescadores. From there they went on to Pangnu Island on the 23rd, and after the men-of-war had bombarded the forts, landed and took possession.

This expedition was probably undertaken to justify the demand which the Japanese were about to make from Li-Hung-Chang for the cession of Formosa and the Pescadores.

Attempted assassination of Li-hung-Chang.

On the 24th March the negotiations were temporarily suspended owing to an attempt on the part of a Japanese fanatic to assassinate the Viceroy. He succeeded in lodging a bullet in Li-Hung-Chang's cheek, but fortunately no serious effects followed.

Armistice arranged.

The Japanese, in order to atone as far as possible for the act itself, and to minimise the effects of the delay in the negotiations, granted an armistice throughout Manchuria, Chihli, and Shantung from the 30th March till the 20th April.

Japanese preparations during negotiations.

The Gulf of Pechihli was now free of ice and the season of rough weather over, and pending the result of the negotiations, the Japanese did not slacken their preparations for landing on the coast of Chihli, and advancing on Peking. Accordingly on the 14th April the Guard and 4th Divisions passed through the Straits of Shimonoseki in fifty transports on their way to Talienwan. H.I.H. Prince Komatsu accompanied them as Commander-in-Chief of the land and sea forces, to establish his headquarters at Port Arthur.

The 2nd Army, consisting of the 2nd, 4th, 6th, and Guard Divisions, was now concentrated in the neighbourhood of Talienwan and Port Arthur; and the 1st and 3rd Divisions of the 1st Army began to move south from Kaiping and Kangwangtsai.

The whole Japanese army could not be transported across the sea simultaneously, and as several trips would be necessary, it was considered simpler to embark all the divisions successively at Port Arthur or Talienwan, where all the necessary provisions and stores had been collected, than to send supplies northwards, and embark the 1st and 3rd Divisions at Yingtzu.

The 5th Division remained in the north to hold the country from Yingtzu to the Yalu.

Chinese preparations.

It was calculated that at this time the Chinese had massed about 200,000 men between Shanhaikuan and

CONCLUSION OF THE WAR.

Peking, in addition to the forces still in Manchuria. These troops had been brought together from the most distant parts of the Empire, but though their numbers were formidable, they could not be expected to make any better stand against the Japanese than those who had already met them.

On the 17th April however, the Treaty of Peace was signed, and the armistice was prolonged until the 8th May, on which day ratifications were exchanged at Chifu, and the war was at an end.

Treaty of peace signed.

By the terms of the treaty the Liaotung peninsula was ceded to Japan. This provision, however, was not carried into effect, and further negotiations were opened with a view to the modification of the terms of peace, and to arranging the withdrawal of the Japanese troops.

Formosa was also ceded to the Japanese, and it was provided that Wei-hai-wei should be held by them pending the payment of the war indemnity.

The following movements of the Japanese troops were therefore carried out:—

The 1st Division returned to Japan at the end of May, followed by the 12th brigade (6th Division), the 3rd Division, and the 5th Division.

The Guard Division was sent to occupy Formosa, and the 11th brigade (6th Division) went to Wei-hai-wei.

The 4th Division occupied the Liaotung peninsula, until finally evacuated, and then reinforced the Guard in Formosa.

APPENDIX A.

Strength and Losses of each Side in the Principal Battles.

		Japanese			Chinese	
		Strength	Killed	Wounded	Strength	Killed
Battles of 1st Army.						
Sŏnghwan (Asan)	29th July	3,500	29	59	3,500	100
Ping Yang	15th Sept.	15,600	189	516	14,000	2,000
Hushan (passage of R. Yalu)	25th Oct.	17,700	34	111	20,000	500
Tsao-ho-kou	25th Nov.	1,420	8	34	6,500	?
N.E. of Tsao-ho-kou	30th ,,	2,550	—	6	2,000	?
Pan-chia-tai	10th Dec.	3,140	11	49	3,500	110
Near Fenghuangchêng	12th ,,	3,590	12	62	4,000	140
,, Hsi-muchêng	11th ,,	2,550	—	8	3,000	70
Kangwangtsai	19th ,,	5,550	69	274	13,000	300
Haicheng	17th Jan.	9,400	3	38	15,000	300
,,	22nd ,,	8,400	8	30	20,000	120
,,	16th Feb.	7,500	3	11	20,000	150
,,	21st ,,	9,800	2	6	20,000	110
Tapingshan	24th ,,	10,000	30	220	17,500	?
N. of Haicheng	28th ,,	12,000	15	109	20,000	400
Niuchwang	4th March	14,200	70	319	5,000	2,000
Tienchuangtai	9th ,,	28,400	16	144	30,000	2,000
Battles of 2nd Army.						
Chinchou	6th Nov.	12,000	None	?	6,000	?
Port Arthur	21st Nov.	15,000	66	353	14,050	2,000
Chinchou	21st ,,	1,500	7	47	8,500	500
Kaiping	10th Jan.	6,700	46	263	4,000	900
Wei-hai-wei	29th Jan. to 1st Feb.	19,000	74	214	6,000	?
Naval Fights.						
Phungtao (Fontao)	25th July	?	None	None	?	?
Hai-yang-tao (Yalu)	17th Sept.	3,823	80	162	?	1,000
Wei-hai-wei	3rd to 11th Feb.	—	27	34	?	?

The total losses in the army up to the 8th June, 1895,* were as follows:—

Killed	...	739
Died of wounds	...	230
,, cholera	...	1,602
,, other diseases	...	1,546
Total deaths	...	**4,117**

Wounded	...	3,009
Cholera patients	...	2,689
Invalids from other causes	...	51,164
		56,862

Of the grand total, 60,979, the 1st Army had ... 39,097
,, ,, 2nd ,, ... 19,919
,, ,, detachments had ... 1,963

* Exclusive of losses in Formosa.

APPENDIX B.

EXPENDITURE OF AMMUNITION BY JAPANESE INFANTRY IN THE PRINCIPAL BATTLES.

		Rounds per man.	
Sönghwan	9th brigade	25	
Ping Yang	11th regiment	18	
	21st „	55	(in 5½ companies).*
	Sakriöng detachment	18	
	1st battalion, 18th regiment	44	
	2nd „ „	26	
	3rd „ „	20	
Hushan	3rd Division	30	
	5th „	26	
Port Arthur	1st regiment	27	
	2nd „	8·6	
	3rd „	4·8	
	3rd battalion, 24th regiment	30	
	14th regiment	21	
Kaiping	1st brigade	27	
Tapingshan	1st Division	27	
Niuchwang	3rd „	13	
	5th „	6·5	
Wei-hai-wei	2nd „	1·6	
	6th „	14	

* Of these, 2 or 3 companies expended nearly 100 rounds per man.

APPENDIX C.

Expenditure of Ammunition by the Japanese Artillery in the Principal Battles.

	Number of guns in action.	Duration of fighting.	Common shell.	Shrapnel shell.	Total.	
Ping-yang.—Sakriöng detachment	6 guns	4 hours	63	280	343	
Oshima's brigade	14 ,,	8 ,,	321	1,128	1,449	Also 12 case shot
Hushan.—3rd Division	24 ,,	3 ,,	83	251	334	
5th ,,	6 ,,	3 ,,	—	45	45	
Corps artillery	6 ,,	3 ,,	39	23	62	
,,	12 mortars	3 ,,	—	53	53	
Port Arthur.—1st Division	36 guns	2 ,,	229	1,431	1,660	
Hasegawa's brigade	6 ,,	1 hour	33	164	197	
Left column	6 ,,	½ ,,	38	—	38	
Siege artillery	30 pieces	1 ,,	73	22	95	
Kaiping	12 guns	2 hours	7	570	577	
Tapingshan	24 ,,	3 ,,	94	1,223	1,317	
Tienchuangtai	84 ,,	3 ,,	437	2,289	2,726	
,,	7 mortars	3 ,,	109	3	112	
Wei-hai-wei.—2nd Division	36 guns	2 ,,	114	113	227	
6th ,,	12 ,,	3 ,,	121	1,022	1,143	

ORDER OF BATTLE OF THE JAPANESE LAND FORCES—continued.

2nd portion (mobilised December 1894).

2ND DIVISION.

Lieutenant-General Sakuma.

3rd Brigade.

Major-General Yamaguchi.
4th Infantry regiment,
16th " "

2nd Cavalry battalion.
2nd Artillery regiment.
2nd Engineer battalion.

4th Brigade.

Major-General Prince Fushimi.
5th Infantry regiment.
17th " "

6TH DIVISION.

11th Brigade.

Major-General Oiela.
13th Infantry regiment.
23rd " "

6th Cavalry battalion, 1 squadron.
6th Artillery regiment, 4 field batteries.
6th Engineer battalion, 1 company.

3rd portion (mobilised February, 1895*).

Siege artillery.
6 9-cm. mortars.

IMPERIAL GUARD.

Lieutenant-General Prince Kitashirakawa.

1st Brigade.

1st Guard infantry regiment,
2nd " " "

2nd Brigade.

3rd Guard infantry regiment,
4th " " "

Guard cavalry battalion.
Guard artillery regiment.
Guard engineer battalion.

4TH DIVISION.

Lieutenant-General Yamazawa.

7th Brigade.

7th Infantry regiment.
8th " "

8th Brigade.

10th Infantry regiment,
20th " "

4th Cavalry battalion.
4th Artillery regiment.
4th Engineer battalion.

Note.—Each Division has, in addition to the above, pontoon trains, supply and ammunition columns, and hospital and field telegraph detachments.

* The Guard was mobilized in October, 1894, but was not moved to Hiroshima until February, 1895.

www.ingramcontent.com/pod-product-compliance
Lightning Source LLC
Chambersburg PA
CBHW032134090426
42743CB00007B/595